Counting by 3s

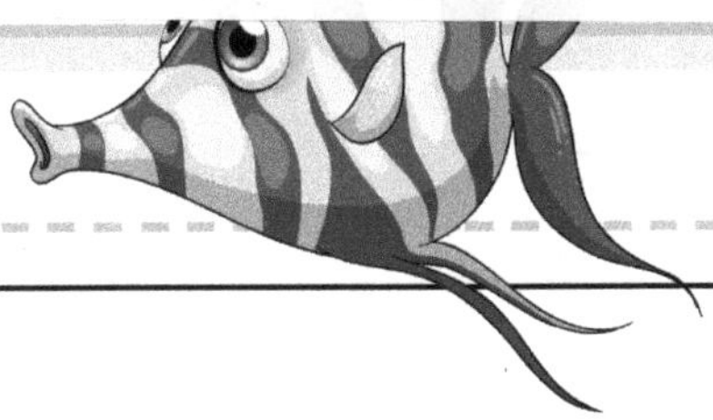

Count by 3s.

1.	6, __9__, ______, ______, ______, ______, ______
2.	24, ______, ______, ______, ______, ______, ______
3.	63, ______, ______, ______, ______, ______, ______
4.	42, ______, ______, ______, ______, ______, ______
5.	84, ______, ______, ______, ______, ______

Count back by 3s.

6.	45, __42__, ______, ______, ______, ______, ______
7.	18, ______, ______, ______, ______, ______, ______
8.	69, ______, ______, ______, ______, ______, ______
9.	99, ______, ______, ______, ______, ______, ______
10.	39, ______, ______, ______, ______, ______, ______

Counting by 4s

Count by 4s.

1.	8, __12__, ____, ____, ____, ____, ____
2.	52, ____, ____, ____, ____, ____, ____
3.	76, ____, ____, ____, ____, ____, ____
4.	68, ____, ____, ____, ____, ____, ____
5.	. 32, ____, ____, ____, ____, ____ ____

Count back by 4s.

6.	56, __52__, ____, ____, ____, ____, ____
7.	76, ____, ____, ____, ____, ____, ____
8.	24, ____, ____, ____, ____, ____, ____
9.	100, ____, ____, __88__, ____, ____, ____
10.	44, ____, ____, ____, ____, ____, ____

Counting by 5s and 25s

Count by 5s.

1.	0, **5**, ______, ______, ______, ______, ______
2.	35, ______, ______, ______, ______, ______, ______
3.	70, ______, ______, ______, ______, ______, ______

Count back by 5s.

4.	35, ______, ______, **20**, ______, ______, ______
5.	100, ______, ______, ______, ______, ______, ______
6.	70, ______, ______, ______, ______, ______, ______

Count by 25s.

7.	25, **50**, ______, ______, ______, ______, ______
8.	200, ______, ______, ______, ______, ______, ______

Count back by 25s.

9.	325, **300**, ______, ______, ______, ______, ______

Counting by 10s

Count by 10s.

1.	20, ______, ______, ______, **60**, ______, ______
2.	33, ______, ______, ______, ______, ______, ______
3.	224, ______, ______, ______, ______, ______, ______
4.	49, ______, ______, ______, ______, ______, ______
5.	130, ______, ______, ______, ______, ______, ______

Count back by 10s.

6.	100, ______, ______, ______, ______, ______, ______
7.	81, ______, ______, ______, ______, ______, ______
8.	168, ______, ______, ______, ______, ______, ______

BRAIN STRETCH

A box has 10 snack bars. Write how many snack bars are in

a) 2 boxes ______ b) 3 boxes ______ c) 5 boxes ______ d) 7 boxes ______

Counting by 100s

Count by 100s.

1.	100, **200**, ______, ______, ______, ______, ______
2.	302, ______, ______, **602**, ______, ______, ______
3.	215, ______, ______, ______, ______, ______, ______
4.	127, ______, ______, ______, ______, ______, ______
5.	348, ______, ______, ______, ______, ______ ______

Count back by 100s.

6.	900, ______, ______, ______, ______, ______, ______
7.	743, ______, ______, ______, ______, ______, ______
8.	619, ______, ______, ______, ______, ______, ______

BRAIN STRETCH

There are 100 jelly beans in one bag. Write how many jelly beans are in

a) 3 bags ______ b) 5 bags ______ c) 10 bags ______

Counting Back by 5s

Start at 100. Connect the dots counting back by 5s.

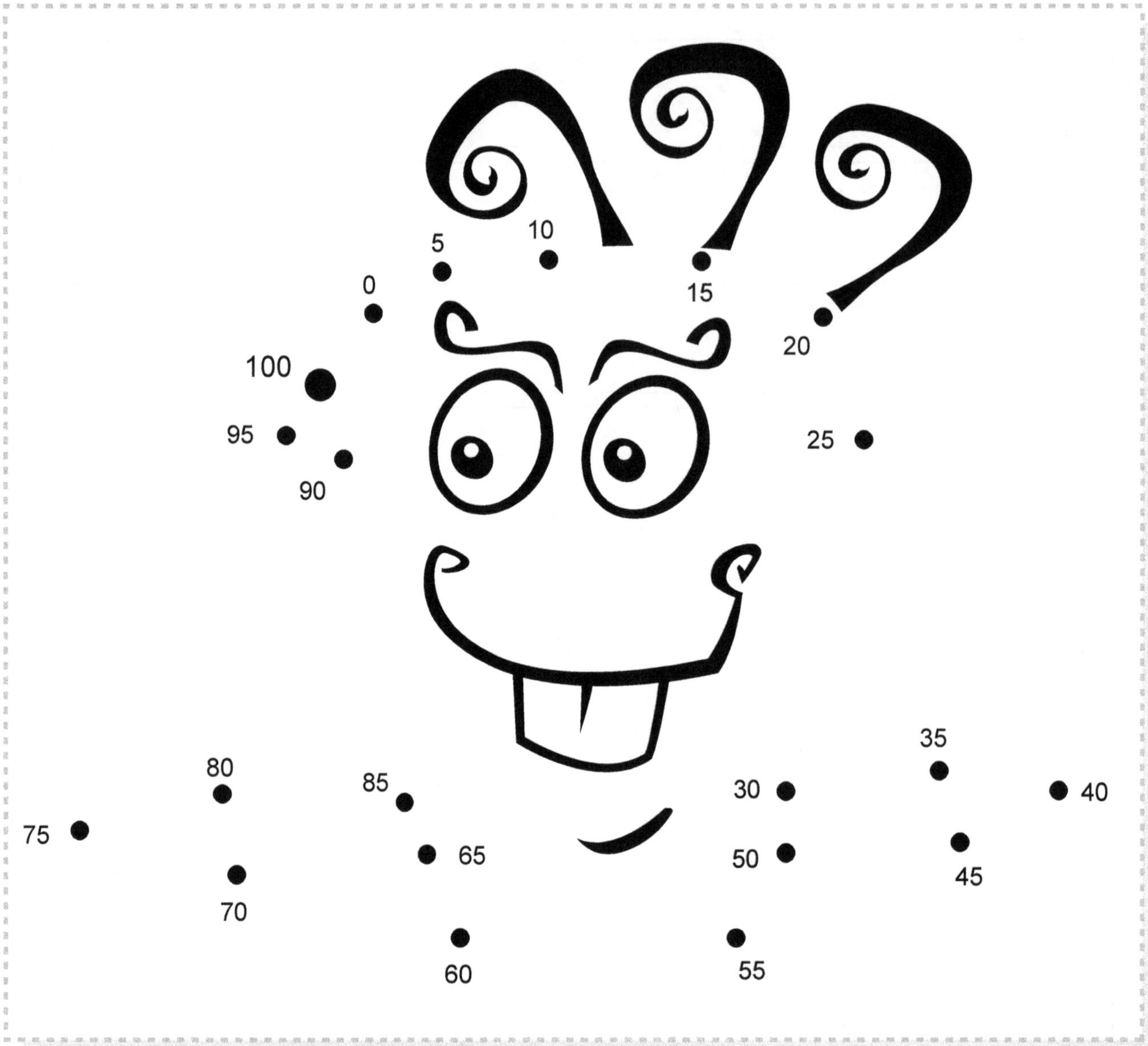

5
10
0
15
20
100
95
25
90
35
80
85
30
40
75
65
50
45
70
60
55

BRAIN STRETCH

Ellie was counting by 3s or 4s and made a mistake.
What mistake did she make?

a) 44, 48, 50, 54 b) 96, 93, 90, 88 c) 72, 68, 64, 61

Counting by 25s to 1000

Connect the dots counting by 25s to 1000.

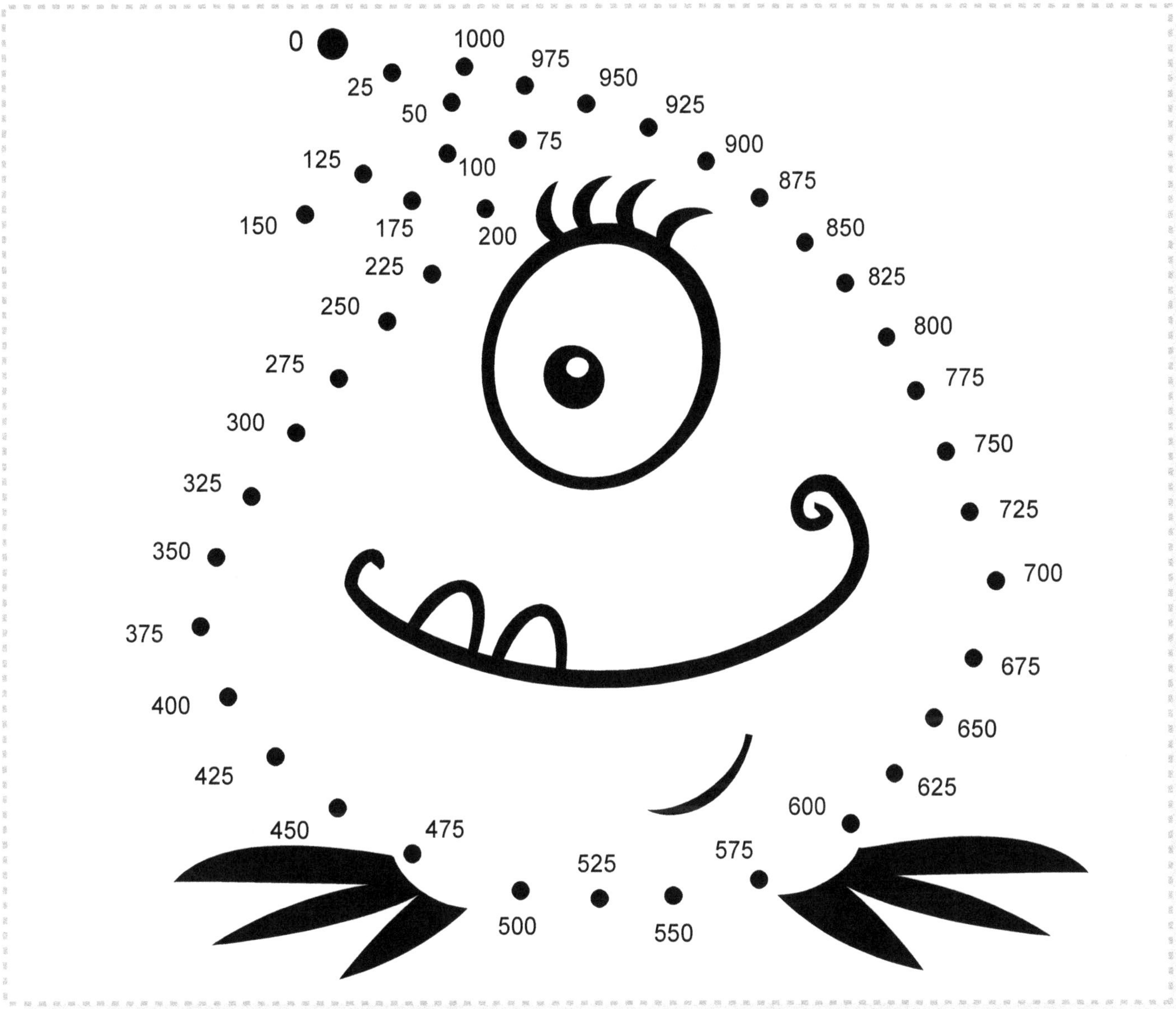
0
25
50
75
100
125
150
175
200
225
250
275
300
325
350
375
400
425
450
475
500
525
550
575
600
625
650
675
700
725
750
775
800
825
850
875
900
925
950
975
1000

BRAIN STRETCH

a) Count back by 5s. 875, _____, _____, _____, _____, _____, _____, _____

b) Count back by 10s. 944, _____, _____, _____, _____, _____, _____, _____

Growing Number Patterns

In a growing pattern, the number increases.

	+ 3		+ 3		+ 3		+ 3		+ 3		+ 3	
3		6		9		12		15		18		21

The pattern rule is add 3 each time.

Make a growing pattern by adding.

1. The pattern rule is add 4 each time.

   8, _______, _______, _______, _______, _______, _______, _______

2. The pattern rule is add 5 each time.

   15, _______, _______, _______, _______, _______, _______, _______

3. The pattern rule is add 10 each time.

   5, _______, _______, _______, _______, _______, _______, _______

4. Make your own. The pattern rule is add ______ each time.

   6, _______, _______, _______, _______, _______, _______, _______

Shrinking Number Patterns

In a shrinking pattern, the number decreases.

	−4		−4		−4		−4		−4		−4	
32		28		24		20		16		12		8

The pattern rule is subtract 4 each time.

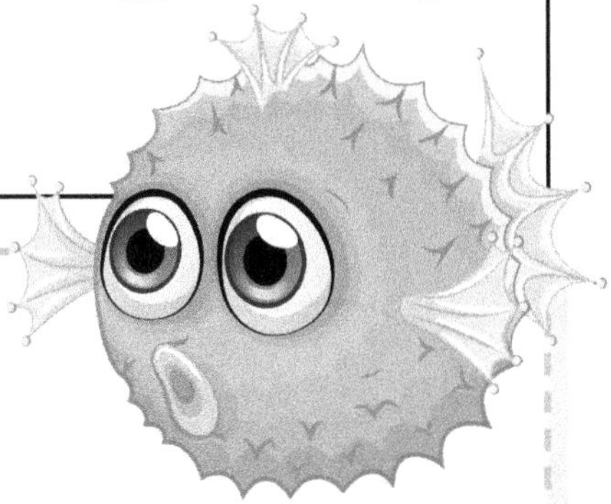

Make a shrinking pattern by subtracting.

1. The pattern rule is subtract 3 each time.

   30, ______, ______, ______, ______, ______, ______, ______

2. The pattern rule is subtract 5 each time.

   45, ______, ______, ______, ______, ______, ______, ______

3. The pattern rule is subtract 10 each time.

   90, ______, ______, ______, ______, ______, ______, ______

4. Make your own. The pattern rule is subtract ______ each time.

   25, ______, ______, ______, ______, ______, ______, ______

Odd and Even Numbers

Look at the ones digits to see if a number is odd or even.
Odd numbers end in 1, 3, 5 , 7, or 9.
Even numbers end in 0, 2, 4, 6, or 8.

Colour the even numbers orange. Colour the odd numbers green.

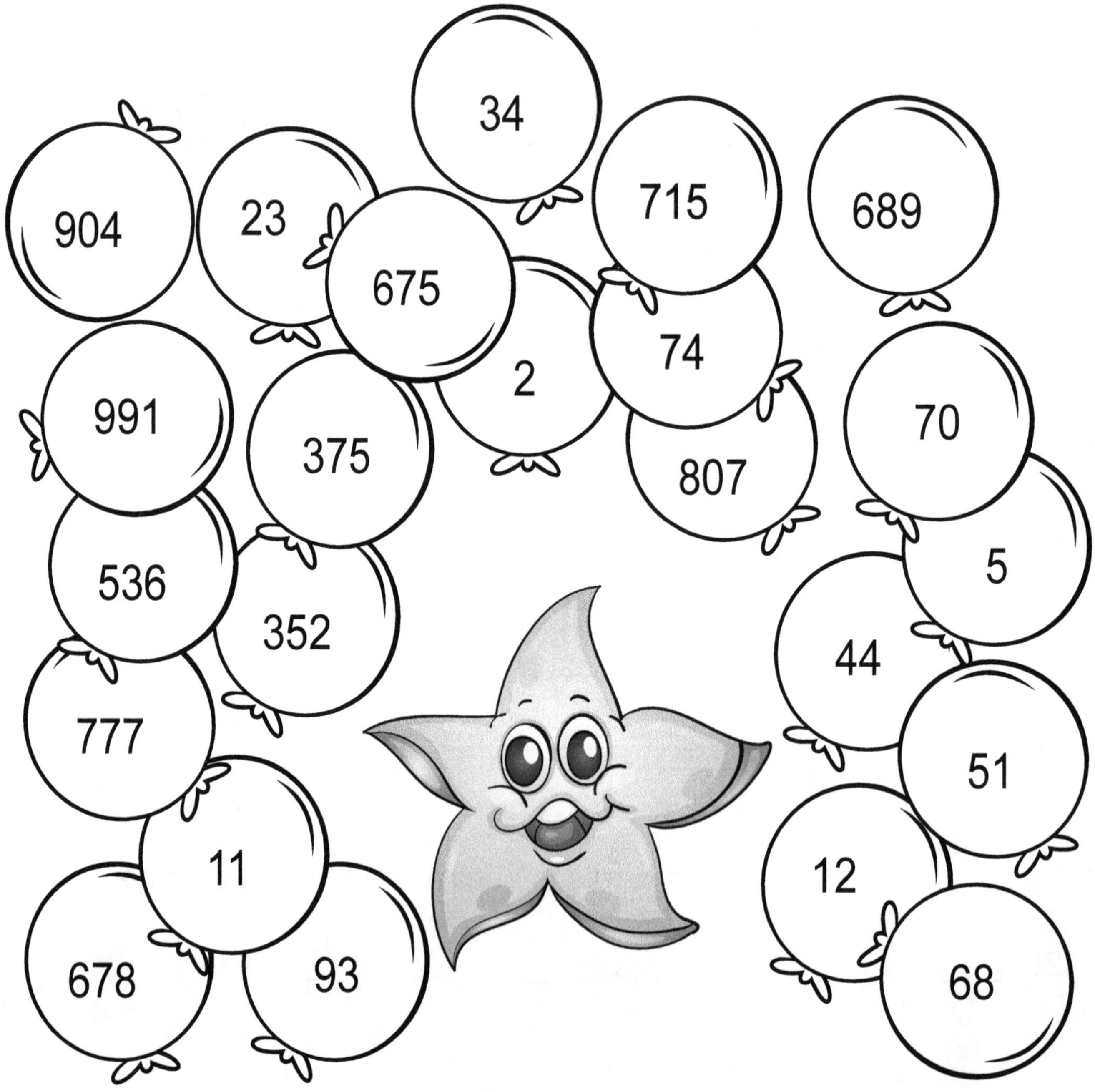
34
904
23
675
715
689
2
74
991
375
807
70
536
352
5
44
777
51
11
12
678
93
68

Comparing and Ordering Numbers

1. Count by 10s. Fill in the missing numbers.

Just before: **71**, 81, 91	Just before: ____, 65, 75
Just after: 2, 12, ____	Just before and after: ____, 89, ____
Between: 14, ____, 34	Just after: 16, 26, ____

2. Circle the larger number in each pair.

a) 231 or 132 b) 334 or 345 c) 128 or 129 d) 236 or 320

e) 537 or 527 f) 435 or 456 g) 954 or 959 h) 211 or 222

3. Order each group of numbers from smallest to largest.

154, 129, 171, 118, 127, 111 ____, ____, ____, ____, ____, ____

339, 363, 30, 384, 317, 400 ____, ____, ____, ____, ____, ____

4. Order each group of numbers from largest to smallest.

95, 84, 123 ____, ____, ____

245, 212, 289 ____, ____, ____

Hundreds, Tens, and Ones

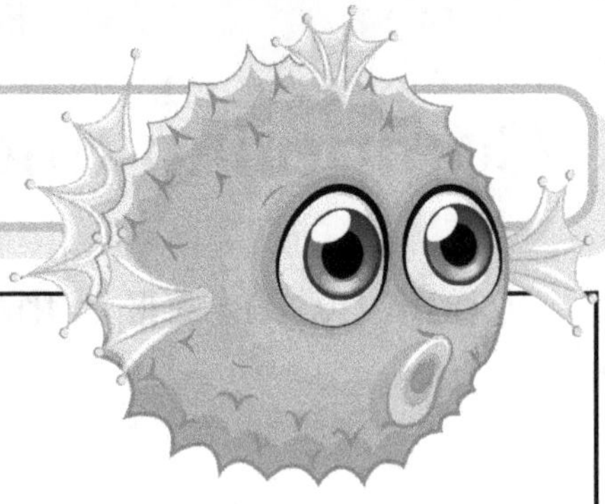

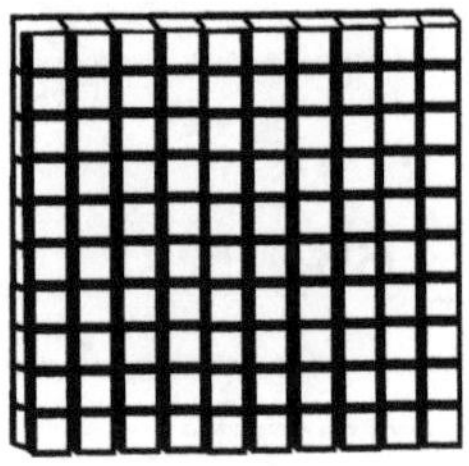 = 100  = 10  = 1

1 hundred + 1 ten + 1 one = 111

Count the hundreds, tens, and ones. Write how many blocks in all.

1. 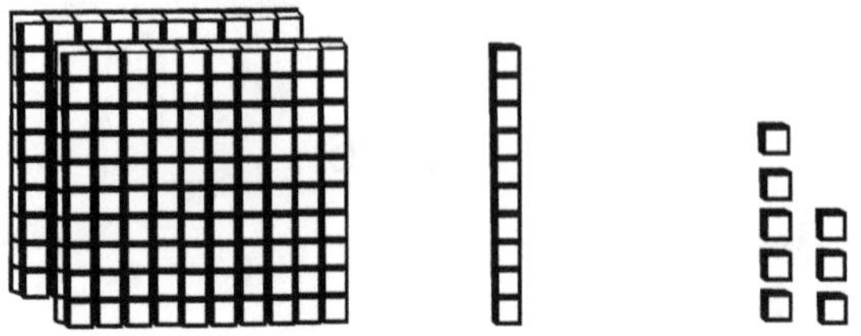

___ hundreds + ___ tens + ___ ones

Number ____

2. 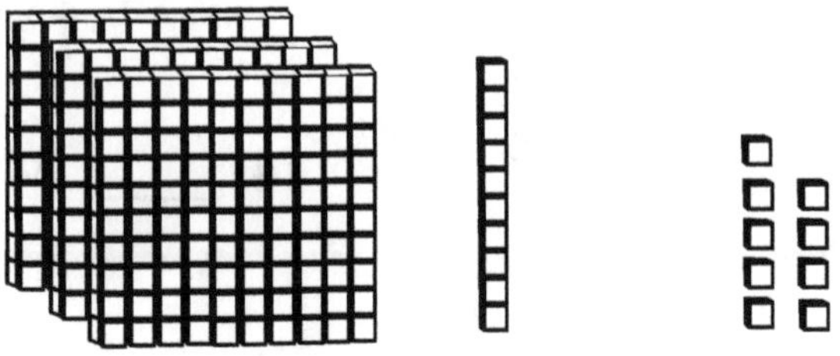

___ hundreds + ___ tens + ___ ones

Number ____

3. 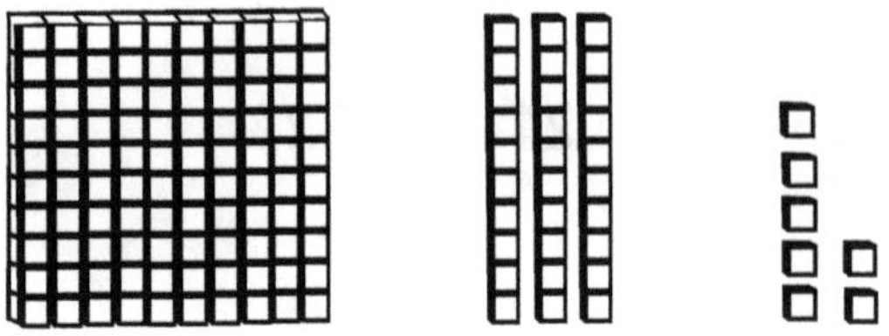

___ hundreds + ___ tens + ___ ones

Number ____

4. 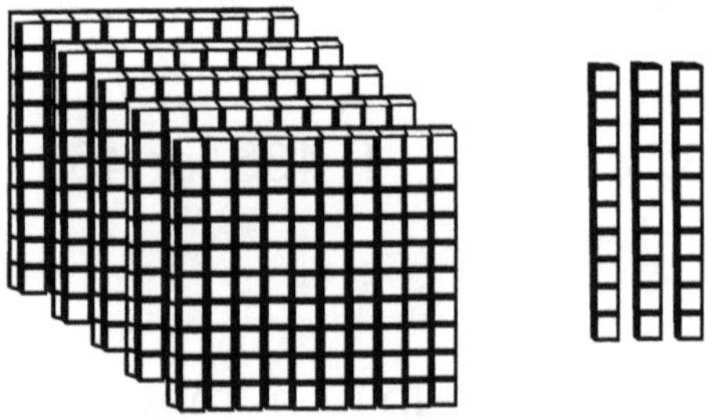

___ hundreds + ___ tens + ___ ones

Number ____

5. 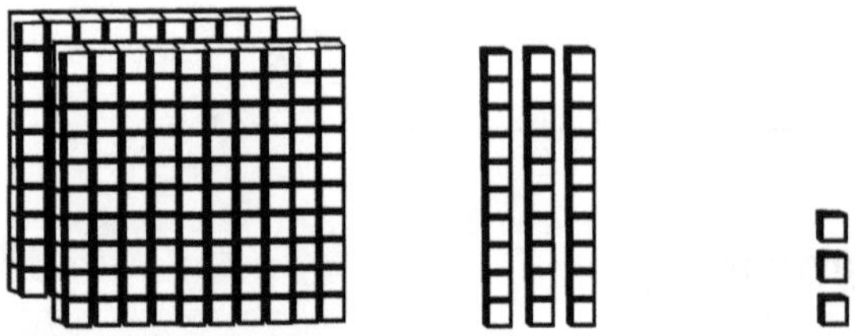

___ hundreds + ___ tens + ___ ones

Number ____

6. 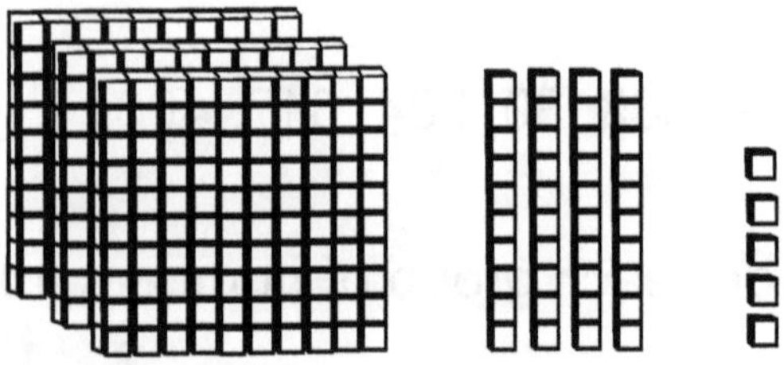

___ hundreds + ___ tens + ___ ones

Number ____

Hundreds, Tens, and Ones (continued)

Count the hundreds, tens, and ones. Write how many blocks in all.

7. 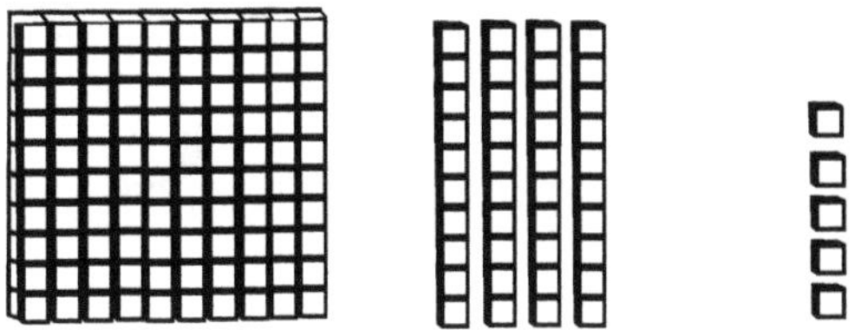

___ hundreds + ___ tens + ___ ones

Number ____

8. 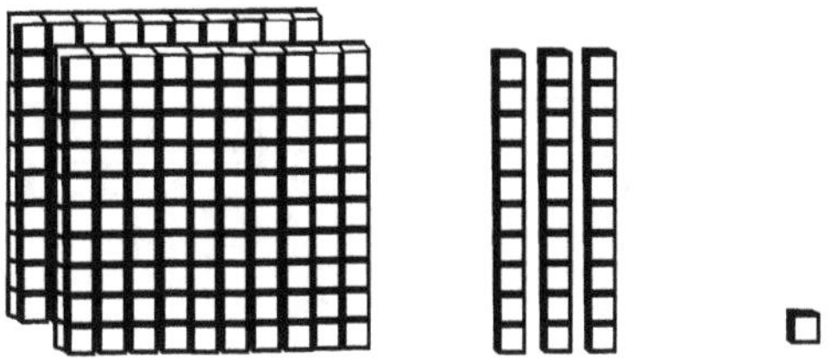

___ hundreds + ___ tens + ___ ones

Number ____

9. 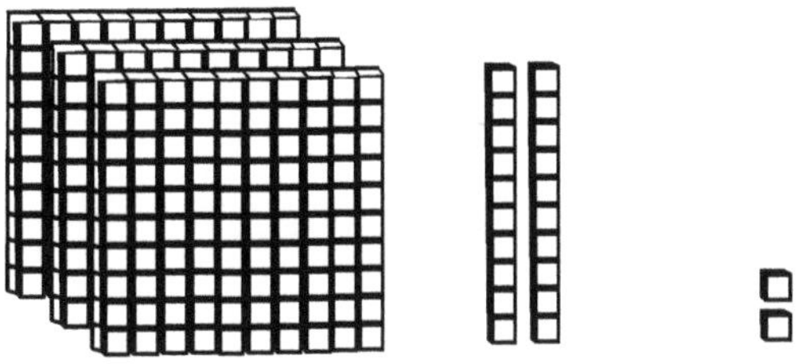

___ hundreds + ___ tens + ___ ones

Number ____

10. 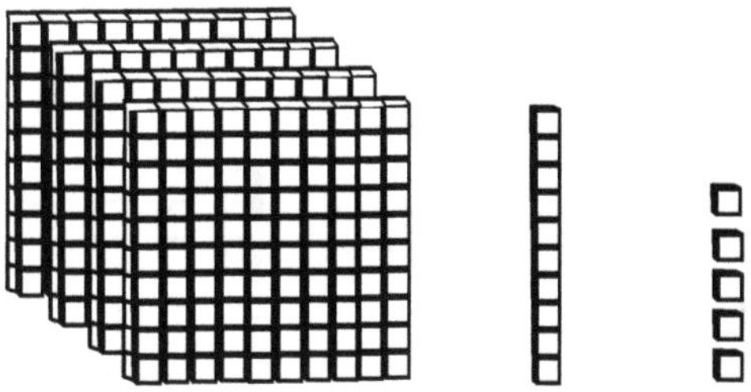

___ hundreds + ___ tens + ___ ones

Number ____

11. 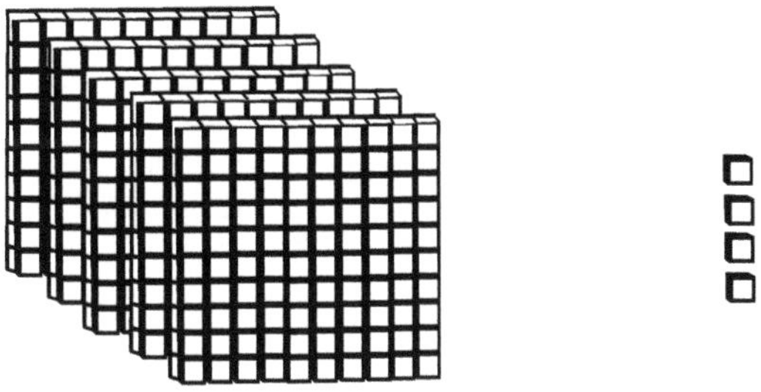

___ hundreds + ___ tens + ___ ones

Number ____

12. 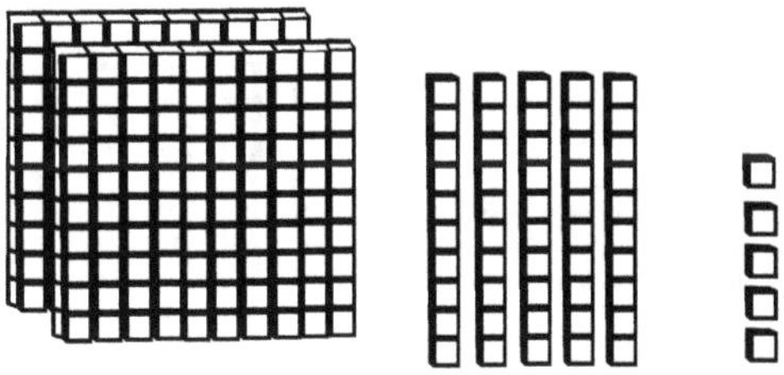

___ hundreds + ___ tens + ___ ones

Number ____

BRAIN STRETCH

Circle the larger number in each set.

a) 132 149

b) 118 128

c) 272 289

d) 459 475

Writing the Number

Count the hundreds, tens, and ones. Write how many blocks in all.

1.

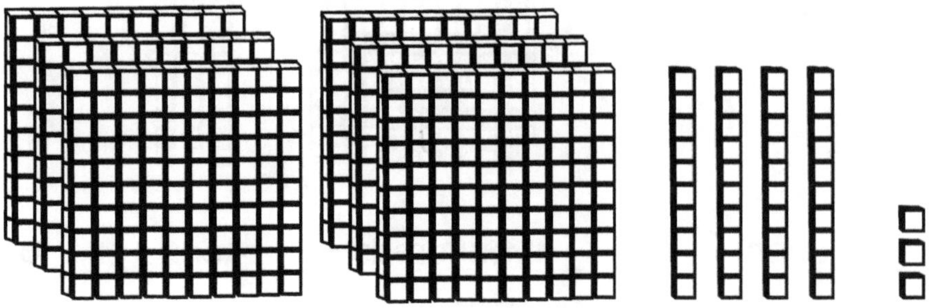

______ hundreds + ______ tens + ______ ones Number ____________

2.

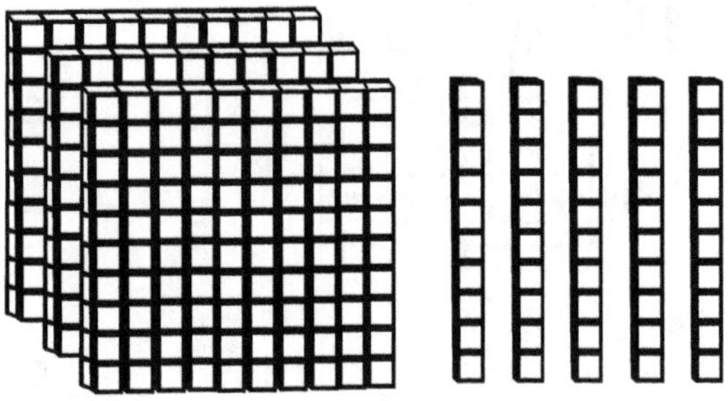

______ hundreds + ______ tens + ______ ones Number ____________

3.

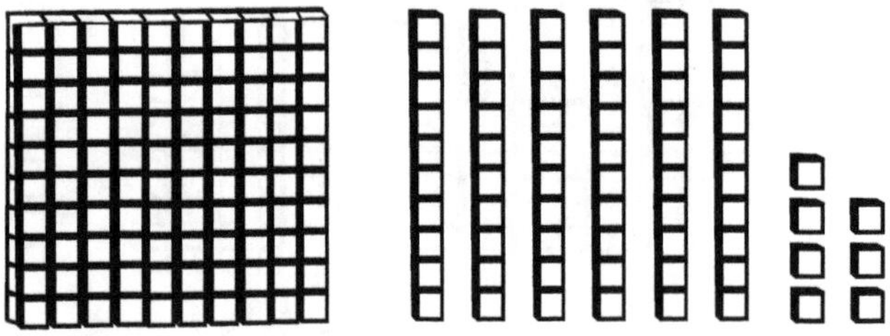

______ hundreds + ______ tens + ______ ones Number ____________

4.

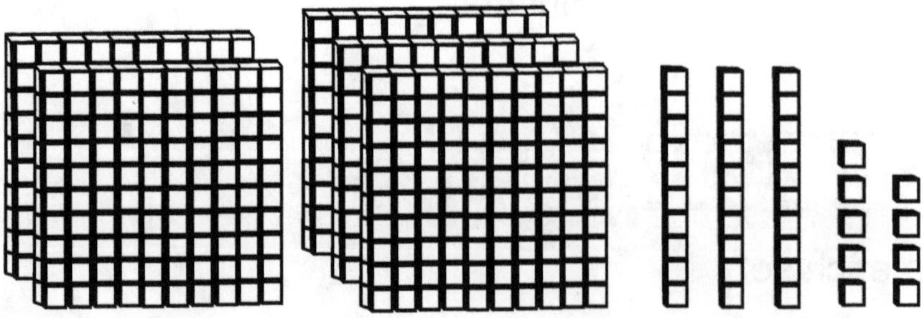

______ hundreds + ______ tens + ______ ones Number ____________

Place Value

For the number 725,

7 stands for 700
2 stands for 20
5 stands for 5

725 in expanded form is 700 + 20 + 5.

Write the place value of the underlined digit.

1. 565 **500**
2. 721 ____________________
3. 428 ____________________
4. 286 ____________________
5. 214 ____________________
6. 673 ____________________
7. 526 ____________________
8. 622 ____________________

Write each number in expanded form.

9. 476 ____________________
10. 258 ____________________
11. 967 ____________________

What Is the Value?

Write the missing value.

1. 500 + 20 + ______________ = 529

2. ______________ hundreds + 2 tens + 4 ones = 324

3. 600 + 80 + ______________ = 681

4. ______________ hundreds + 0 tens + 4 ones = 704

5. 600 + ______________ + 7 = 647

6. 7 hundreds + ______________ tens + 9 ones = 749

7. 200 + ______________ + 6 = 276

8. 8 hundreds + 6 tens + ______________ ones = 862

BRAIN STRETCH

Compare and write >, <, or =.

a) 804 ______ 728

b) 430 ______ 375

c) 664 ______ 668

d) 179 ______ 199

Writing Numbers in Different Ways

Circle two correct ways to make each number.

1. 141	**140** + **1**	**1** hundred and **1** ten and **4** ones	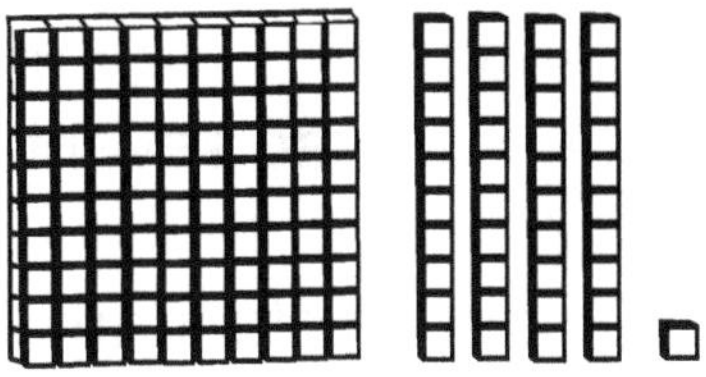	
2. 229	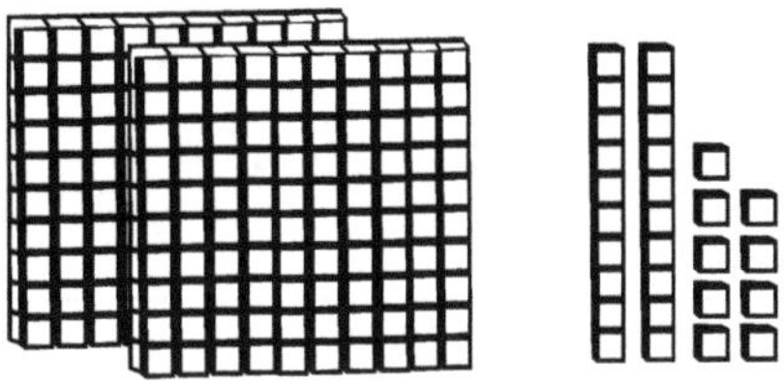	**2** hundreds and **2** tens and **9** ones	**200** + **2** + **9**	
3. 316	**3** hundreds and **1** ten and **6** ones	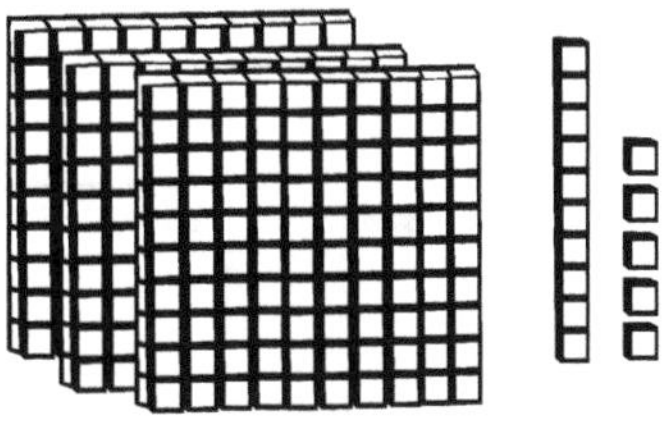	**300** + **10** + **6**	
4. 153	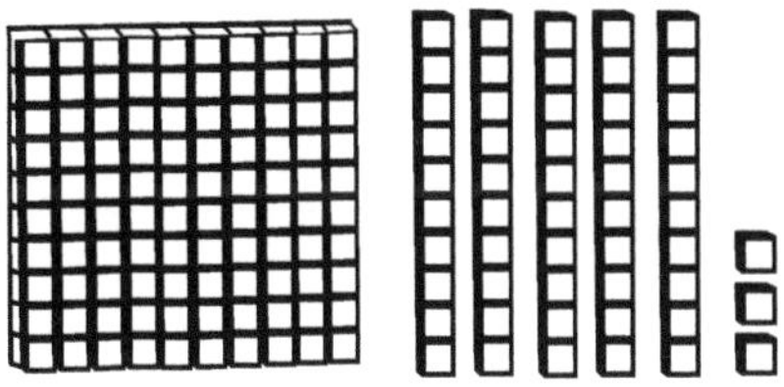	**1** hundred and **5** tens and **3** ones	**100** + **30** + **5**	
5. 290	**2** hundreds and **9** tens and **0** ones	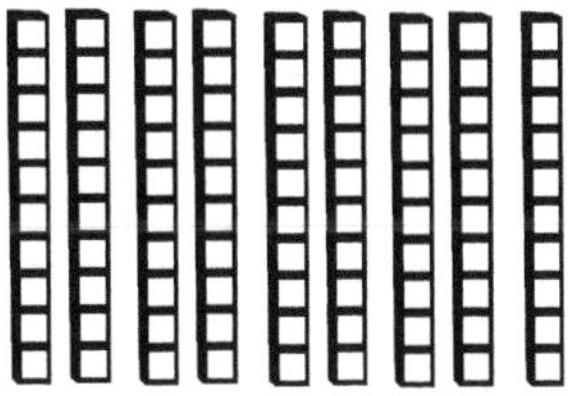	**200** + **90** + **0**	
6. 365	**3** hundreds and **6** tens and **5** ones	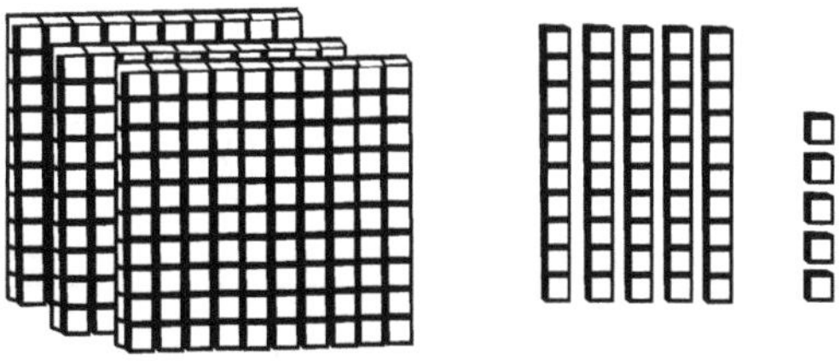	**300** + **60** + **5**	

Writing Numbers in Standard Form

There are different ways to write a number.

100 + 10 + 7
1 hundred + 1 ten + 7 ones
one hundred seventeen
117

117 is written in standard form.

Write each number in standard form.

1.	100 + 40 + 5	______
2.	7 tens 6 ones	______
3.	ninety-two	______
4.	200 + 60 + 2	______
5.	3 hundreds 4 ones	______
6.	two hundred eleven	______
7.	800 + 50 + 6	______
8.	eighty	______
9.	6 hundreds 5 tens	______
10.	forty-five	______
11.	4 hundreds 3 tens 9 ones	______
12.	500 + 80 + 3	______

Writing Number Words

Number words for the teens:
eleven twelve thirteen fourteen fifteen sixteen seventeen eighteen nineteen

Number words for the tens:
twenty thirty forty fifty sixty seventy eighty ninety

The number word for 285 is two hundred eighty-five.

1. Write the number word.

   a) 121 **one hundred twenty-one**

   b) 234 ______________________________

   c) 456 ______________________________

   d) 139 ______________________________

   e) 918 ______________________________

2. Write the number word.

   a) There are ____________ months in one year.
   12

   b) There are ____________ weeks in a year.
   52

   c) There are ____________ days in a year.
   365

   d) Some months of the year have ____________ days.
   30

   Other months have ____________ days.
   31

   e) There are ____________ hours in a day.
   24

   f) There are ____________ minutes in one hour.
   60

Number Round Up

To round to the nearest tens place, look at the ones digit.
If the ones digit has a 0, 1, 2, 3, or 4, round down.
If the ones digit has a 5, 6, 7, 8, or 9, round up.

To round to the nearest hundreds place, look at the tens digit.
If the tens digit has a 0, 1, 2, 3, or 4, round down.
If the tens digit has a 5, 6, 7, 8, or 9, round up.

Round each number.

	Number	Round to nearest 10	Round to nearest 100
1.	673		
2.	102		
3.	837		
4.	109		
5.	651		
6.	722		
7.	574		
8.	450		
9.	498		
10.	813		

Ordinal Numbers

An ordinal number tells the position of something in a list.

1. Write the ordinals. Hint: Use the **bold** part to help you.

   fir**st** __1st__ seco**nd** __________ thi**rd** __________

   four**th** __________ fif**th** __________ six**th** __________ seven**th** __________

   eigh**th** __________ nin**th** __________ ten**th** __________

2. What is a) the first letter in the alphabet? ____
   b) the 9th letter in the word "snowboard"? ____
   c) the second letter in the word "hockey"? ____
   d) the 8th letter in the alphabet? ____
   e) the tenth letter in the word "Kapuskasing"? ____

3. Some students had a contest to find out whose paper airplane flew the farthest.
   a) Ben came in tenth. Who came in first? ________
   b) Who came in fourth? ________
   c) In which position was Mandy? ________
   d) In which position was Paul? ________

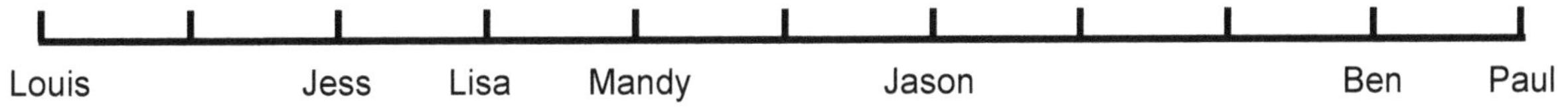
Louis
Jess
Lisa
Mandy
Jason
Ben
Paul

Adding or Subtracting

You can find the sum of two numbers by counting on.
14 + 5 = 19 Count: 14, 15, 16, 17, 18, 19

You can find the difference between two numbers by counting back.
29 – 4 = 25 Count: 29, 28, 27, 26, 25

Use the number line to help find the sum or difference.

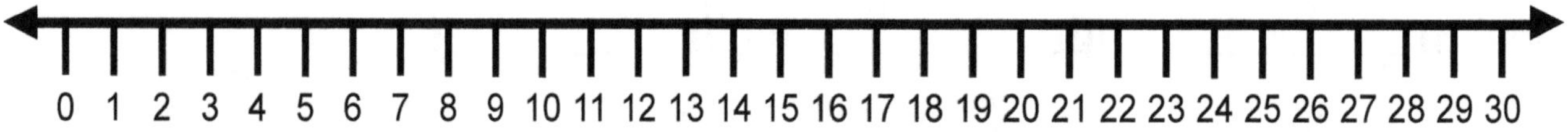
0 1 2 3 4 5 6 7 8 9 10 11 12 13 14 15 16 17 18 19 20 21 22 23 24 25 26 27 28 29 30

26 + 3 = ☐	17 + 2 = ☐	16 – 5 = ☐
27 – 5 = ☐	18 + 9 = ☐	18 + 2 = ☐
16 – 3 = ☐	29 – 8 = ☐	22 + 6 = ☐
16 + 5 = ☐	30 – 5 = ☐	19 – 1 = ☐
18 + 7 = ☐	15 + 7 = ☐	11 – 4 = ☐
28 – 9 = ☐	2 + 25 = ☐	13 – 7 = ☐

Three-Digit Addition Without Regrouping

Line up the ones, tens, and hundreds.

Add the ones.

hundreds	tens	ones
2	2	3
+ 3	4	5
		8

Next add the tens.

hundreds	tens	ones
2	2	3
+ 3	4	5
	6	8

Then add the hundreds.

hundreds	tens	ones
2	2	3
+ 3	4	5
5	6	8

1. Use a hundreds, tens, and ones chart to help add. Shade the ones column yellow. Shade the tens column orange. Shade the hundreds column green.

$$\begin{array}{r} 454 \\ +\ 231 \\ \hline \end{array} \quad \begin{array}{r} 122 \\ +\ 515 \\ \hline \end{array} \quad \begin{array}{r} 371 \\ +\ 327 \\ \hline \end{array} \quad \begin{array}{r} 135 \\ +\ 762 \\ \hline \end{array} \quad \begin{array}{r} 844 \\ +\ 130 \\ \hline \end{array}$$

$$\begin{array}{r} 412 \\ +\ 550 \\ \hline \end{array} \quad \begin{array}{r} 376 \\ +\ 412 \\ \hline \end{array} \quad \begin{array}{r} 462 \\ +\ 223 \\ \hline \end{array} \quad \begin{array}{r} 284 \\ +\ 311 \\ \hline \end{array} \quad \begin{array}{r} 933 \\ +\ \ 13 \\ \hline \end{array}$$

$$\begin{array}{r} 154 \\ +\ 833 \\ \hline \end{array} \quad \begin{array}{r} 231 \\ +\ 426 \\ \hline \end{array} \quad \begin{array}{r} 553 \\ +\ 311 \\ \hline \end{array} \quad \begin{array}{r} 762 \\ +\ 137 \\ \hline \end{array} \quad \begin{array}{r} 114 \\ +\ 630 \\ \hline \end{array}$$

$$\begin{array}{r} 482 \\ +\ 315 \\ \hline \end{array} \quad \begin{array}{r} 612 \\ +\ 340 \\ \hline \end{array} \quad \begin{array}{r} 334 \\ +\ 114 \\ \hline \end{array} \quad \begin{array}{r} 220 \\ +\ 613 \\ \hline \end{array} \quad \begin{array}{r} 152 \\ +\ 543 \\ \hline \end{array}$$

Three-Digit Addition Without Regrouping (continued)

2. Use the hundreds, tens, and ones chart to add. Shade the ones column yellow. Shade the tens column orange. Shade the hundreds column green.

133 + 14 ____	655 + 130 ____	213 + 500 ____	155 + 323 ____	172 + 325 ____
314 + 43 ____	723 + 225 ____	377 + 111 ____	432 + 422 ____	424 + 532 ____
235 + 113 ____	472 + 126 ____	263 + 713 ____	254 + 312 ____	545 + 313 ____
421 + 332 ____	116 + 260 ____	585 + 414 ____	543 + 436 ____	611 + 255 ____
353 + 246 ____	345 + 534 ____	634 + 215 ____	815 + 133 ____	882 + 116 ____

Three-Digit Addition with Regrouping

Line up the ones, tens, and hundreds.
Add the ones.
Then add the tens.

If there are more than 9 tens,
trade 10 tens for 1 hundred.
Regroup in the hundreds column.
Write the tens.
Add the hundreds.

	hundreds	tens	ones
	1		
	3	3	6
+	2	9	3
	6	2	9

Trade 10 tens from 120 for 1 hundred.
Regroup by writing 1 in the hundreds column.

1. Use a hundreds, tens and ones chart to help add. Shade the ones column yellow. Shade the tens column orange. Shade the hundreds column green.

564	+ 255	222	+ 491	175	+ 572	439	+ 290	144	+ 183
212	+ 195	376	+ 441	564	+ 271	429	+ 180	636	+ 173
754	+ 175	335	+ 582	125	+ 193	262	+ 353	417	+ 392

Three-Digit Addition with Regrouping (continued)

2. Use the hundreds, tens and ones chart to add. Hint: If there are more than 9 ones, trade 10 ones for 1 ten. Regroup in the tens column.

□1 239 + 412 651	□□ 378 + 319 ___	□□ 464 + 216 ___	□□ 657 + 114 ___	□□ 735 + 119 ___
□□ 236 + 338 ___	□□ 824 + 26 ___	□□ 543 + 229 ___	□□ 727 + 264 ___	□□ 348 + 338 ___
□□ 347 + 419 ___	□□ 717 + 148 ___	□□ 834 + 19 ___	□□ 239 + 431 ___	□□ 555 + 226 ___

3. Add. Regroup in the tens column and the hundreds column.

1 1 379 + 23 402	□□ 287 + 128 ___	□□ 457 + 166 ___	□□ 564 + 257 ___	□□ 676 + 138 ___

Taking Apart to Make Tens for Addition

9 + 5 = 9 + <u>1</u> + <u>4</u> = <u>10</u> + <u>4</u> = <u>14</u>

9 + 1 make 10 4 is left

38 + 5 = 38 + <u>2</u> + <u>3</u> = <u>40</u> + <u>3</u> = <u>43</u>

38 + 2 make 40 3 is left

1. Use tens to add.

a) 8 + 7 = ___ + ___ + ___ = ___ + ___ = ____

b) 25 + 9 = ___ + ___ + ___ = ___ + ___ = ____

2. Use tens to add. Show your work.

a) 34 + 7 =

b) 49 + 4 =

c) 73 + 8

d) 59 + 5 =

e) 48 + 13 =

f) 65 + 15 =

Three-Digit Subtraction Without Regrouping

Line up the ones, tens, and hundreds.

Subtract the ones.

hundreds	tens	**ones**
4	8	7
− 1	4	4
		3

Then subtract the tens.

hundreds	**tens**	ones
4	8	7
− 1	4	4
	4	3

Then subtract the hundreds.

hundreds	tens	ones
4	8	7
− 1	4	4
3	4	3

1. Use a hundreds, tens, and ones chart to help subtract. Shade the ones column yellow. Shade the tens column orange. Shade the hundreds column green.

358 − 111	487 − 243	129 − 13	274 − 130	633 − 312
578 − 123	696 − 432	584 − 372	367 − 223	985 − 514
849 − 527	767 − 241	425 − 315	246 − 135	536 − 516
486 − 31	943 − 741	398 − 323	572 − 421	433 − 130

Three-Digit Subtraction Without Regrouping (continued)

2. Use the hundreds, tens, and ones chart to subtract.

248 − 236 = ____	836 − 120 = ____	576 − 134 = ____	128 − 114 = ____	695 − 431 = ____
167 − 40 = ____	389 − 232 = ____	645 − 320 = ____	273 − 60 = ____	283 − 73 = ____
324 − 110 = ____	442 − 341 = ____	457 − 312 = ____	839 − 623 = ____	765 − 450 = ____
445 − 234 = ____	198 − 125 = ____	686 − 343 = ____	377 − 225 = ____	985 − 122 = ____

BRAIN STRETCH

Use blocks to subtract 238 – 125. Draw a picture to show your work.

Subtraction Match

Match the question and the answer.

$\begin{array}{r} 245 \\ -\ 131 \\ \hline \end{array}$	667
$\begin{array}{r} 396 \\ -\ 252 \\ \hline \end{array}$	103
$\begin{array}{r} 697 \\ -\ 30 \\ \hline \end{array}$	431
$\begin{array}{r} 528 \\ -\ 212 \\ \hline \end{array}$	322
$\begin{array}{r} 473 \\ -\ 222 \\ \hline \end{array}$	316
$\begin{array}{r} 138 \\ -\ 35 \\ \hline \end{array}$	114
$\begin{array}{r} 779 \\ -\ 348 \\ \hline \end{array}$	144
$\begin{array}{r} 484 \\ -\ 162 \\ \hline \end{array}$	251

Taking Apart to Make Tens for Subtraction

31 – ⑥ = 31 + 4 – 6 + 4 = 35 – 10 = 25
6 + 4 = 10 So, add 4 to each number.

1. Use 10 to make an easier problem. Then subtract.

a) 15 – 9 = 15 + **1** – 9 + **1** = ___ – ___ = ___ Add **1** to each number.

b) 13 – 7 = ___ + ___ – ___ + ___ = ___ – ___ = ___ Add ___ to each number.

c) 17 – 8 = ___ + ___ – ___ + ___ = ___ – ___ = ___ Add ___ to each number.

d) 18 – 9 = ___ + ___ – ___ + ___ = ___ – ___ = ___ Add ___ to each number.

e) 43 – 6 = Add ___ to each number.

f) 34 – 5 = Add ___ to each number.

g) 26 – 7 = Add ___ to each number.

Taking Apart to Make Tens for Subtraction (continued)

23 – 18 = 23 + <u>2</u> – 18 + <u>2</u> = 25 – 20 = 5
18 + 2 = 20 So, add 2 to each number.

2. Use 10 to make an easier problem. Then subtract.

a) 34 – 17 = ___ + ___ – ___ + ___ = ___ – ___ = ___ Add ___ to each number.

b) 28 – 19 = ___ + ___ – ___ + ___ = ___ – ___ = ___ Add ___ to each number.

c) 22 – 16 = ___ + ___ – ___ + ___ = ___ – ___ = ___ Add ___ to each number.

d) 34 – 15 = ___ + ___ – ___ + ___ = ___ – ___ = ___ Add ___ to each number.

e) 43 – 35 = Add ___ to each number.

f) 51 – 39 = Add ___ to each number.

g) 35 – 26 = Add ___ to each number.

Three-Digit Subtraction with Regrouping

Line up the ones, tens, and hundreds.
Subtract the ones.

Trade 1 hundred from the hundreds for 10 tens in the tens column.
Subtract the tens.
Then subtract the hundreds.

	hundreds	**tens**	ones
	5	14	
	~~6~~	~~4~~	6
−	3	8	3
	2	6	3

You cannot take 8 from 4. So, trade 1 hundred from the hundreds for 10 tens. Now there are 14 tens.

1. Use a hundreds, tens, and ones chart to help subtract. Shade the ones column yellow. Shade the tens column orange. Shade the hundreds column green.

$466 - 275$ | $317 - 136$ | $635 - 264$ | $556 - 293$ | $429 - 137$

$238 - 158$ | $575 - 385$ | $674 - 494$ | $768 - 487$ | $424 - 242$

$858 - 376$ | $789 - 296$ | $515 - 155$ | $974 - 383$ | $621 - 160$

Three-Digit Subtraction with Regrouping

2. Use the hundreds, tens, and ones chart to subtract.
   You will need to regroup the tens.

□ [3] [10] 4 ~~4~~ ~~0~~ − 129 **311**	□□□ 460 − 165	□□□ 367 − 148	□□□ 242 − 124	□□□ 691 − 176
□□□ 581 − 366	□□□ 230 − 118	□□□ 541 − 234	□□□ 453 − 245	□□□ 380 − 219
□□□ 873 − 314	□□□ 252 − 139	□□□ 692 − 356	□□□ 282 − 137	□□□ 537 − 318

3. Subtract. Regroup in the tens column and the hundreds column.

□□□ 425 − 191	□□□ 639 − 394	□□□ 953 − 316	□□□ 340 − 245	□□□ 532 − 276

Word Problems

Decide if you need to add or subtract. Underline any words that help you decide. Circle Add or Subtract. Then solve the problem. Show your work.

1. Sandra had 125 marbles. She gave 76 to Dave. How many marbles does she have left?

   Add

   Subtract

   There are ________ marbles left.

2. Mrs. Stevens's class had 186 tulip bulbs to plant. The class planted 79 tulip bulbs. How many tulip bulbs still need to be planted?

   Add

   Subtract

   There are ________ tulip bulbs to be planted.

3. Spencer scored 254 points on a computer game. Ben scored 178 points. How many points did they score altogether?

   Add

   Subtract

   They scored ________ points altogether.

4. Michael collected 379 stamps. Maddy collected 314 stamps. How many stamps did they collect altogether?

   Add

   Subtract

   There are ________ stamps in all.

Money Riddle

When does it rain money?

___ $1.25	___ $3.00	___ $2.00	___ $2.50	|	___ 50¢	___ $3.00	___ $2.00	___ $1.20	___ $2.00	|	
___ 25¢	___ $1.50	|	___ $2.35	___ $3.00	___ $1.00	___ $2.50	___ 75¢	___ $2.00	|		
___ 25¢	___ $2.50	|	___ 50¢	___ $3.00	___ $2.00	|					
___ $1.25	___ $2.00	___ $1.00	___ 50¢	___ $3.00	___ $2.00	___ $1.20					

Watch out! Not all the letters are used in the riddle!

A  ______	C  ______	E  ______	G  ______
H  ______	I  ______	N  ______	R  ______
S  ______	T  ______	W  ______	Y  ______

Counting with Coins

Find the value of the coins. Remember to use the $ sign.

1. 
CANADA
2 DOLLARS
CANADA
DOLLAR
CANADA
25 cents

____

2. 
CANADA
2 DOLLARS
CANADA
DOLLAR
CANADA
25 cents

____

3. 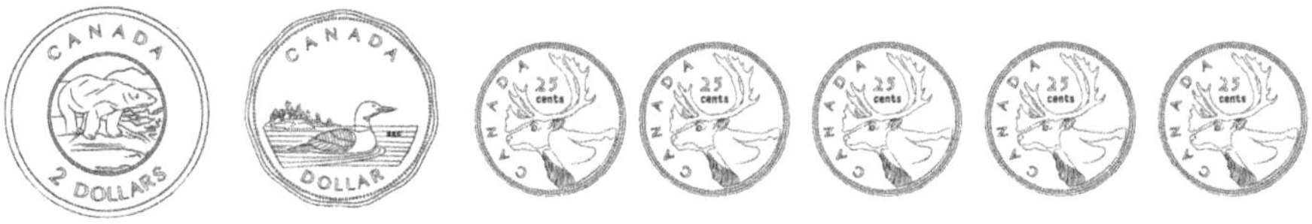
CANADA
2 DOLLARS
CANADA
DOLLAR
CANADA
25 cents

____

4. 
CANADA
2 DOLLARS
CANADA
DOLLAR
CANADA
25 cents

____

5. 
CANADA
2 DOLLARS
CANADA
25 cents

____

Estimating Coins

1.

Estimate $_______.__________ **Count $_______.__________**

2.

Estimate $_______.__________ **Count $_______.__________**

3.

Estimate $_______.__________ **Count $_______.__________**

4.

Estimate $_______.__________ **Count $_______.__________**

Trading Coins

1. Trade each set of coins for fewer coins. Draw the coins. Check your work.

Coin value $1.35

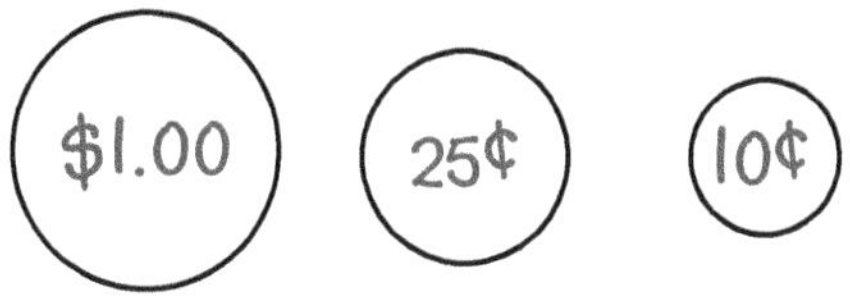
$1.00
25¢
10¢

$1.00 + $0.25 + $0.10 = $1.35

a)

Coin value ________

b)

Coin value ________

c)

Coin value ________

d)

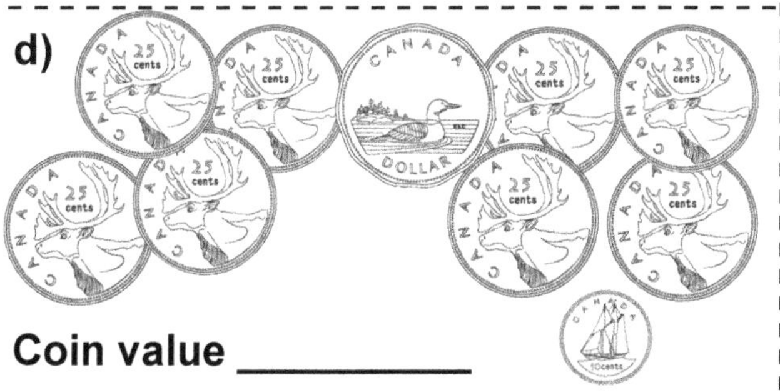

Coin value ________

Comparing Money Values

1. Compare and write >, <, or = in the ◯.

a)

What is the value? ______________

What is the value? ______________

b)

What is the value? ______________

What is the value? ______________

BRAIN STRETCH

Rewrite the amount of money in dollar notation.

1. four dollars and fifty cents ______________
2. nine dollars and forty-five cents ______________
3. two dollars and twenty-five cents ______________

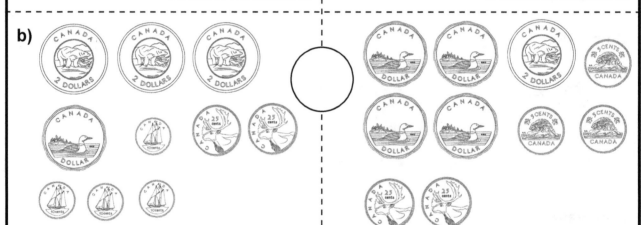

Comparing Money Values (continued)

2. Compare and write >, <, or = in the ◯ .

a)

What is the value? ______________

What is the value? ______________

b)

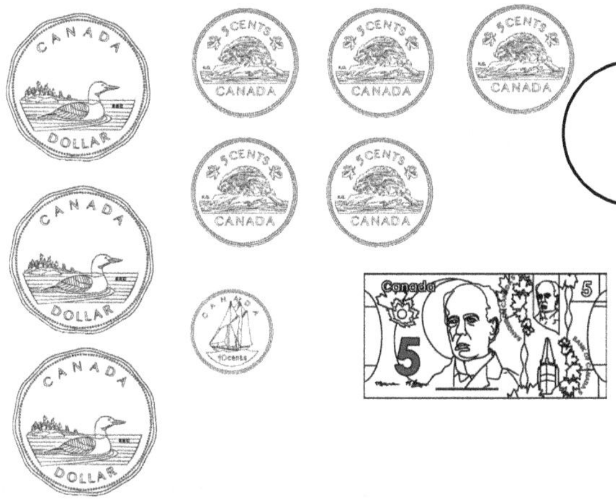

What is the value? ______________

What is the value? ______________

c)

What is the value? ______________

What is the value? ______________

At the Cafeteria

Menu	
Pizza Slice	$1.50
Macaroni and Cheese	$1.80
Sandwich	$1.90
Veggie Sticks	$1.15
Juice	$0.85
Lemonade	$0.95
Milk	$0.90
Jello	$0.65

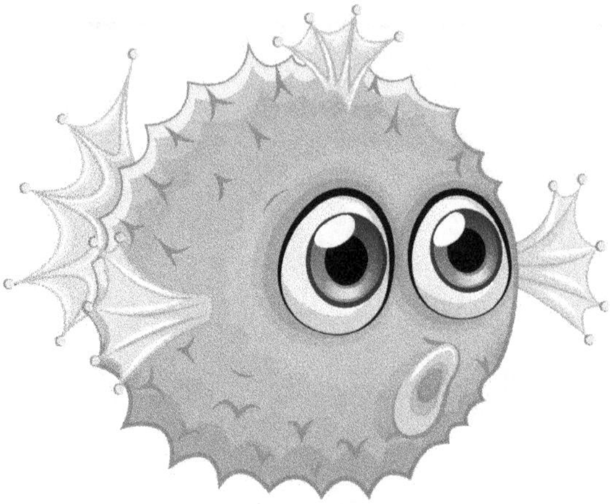

1. Write the prices of the items from least to greatest.

____________ ____________ ____________ ____________

____________ ____________ ____________ ____________

2. a) How much is 1 pizza slice, 1 juice, and 1 jello? __________

   b) Jana has 1 toonie and 1 loonie.
   Does she have enough money to pay? Yes No Show your work.

3. Amin had 2 toonies and 3 quarters to spend for lunch. What could he buy? Calculate his change.

____ _______________

4. What could you buy at the cafeteria if you had $6.00?

____

____

Arrays

In the array, there are 2 rows with 4 blocks in each row.
Skip count by 4s to count the blocks.
The multiplication statement is $2 \times 4 = 8$.

1. Write a multiplication statement for each array.

2 rows and **3** blocks in each row **$2 \times 3 = 6$**

a) 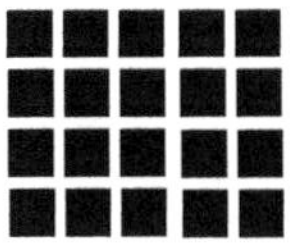

___ rows and ___ blocks in each row ___________

b) 

___ rows and ___ blocks in each row ___________

c) 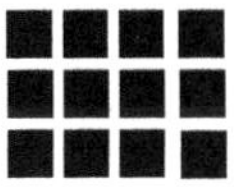

___ rows and ___ blocks in each row ___________

2. Write a multiplication statement for each array.

a)  ___________

b)  ___________

c)  ___________

d)  ___________

Arrays (continued)

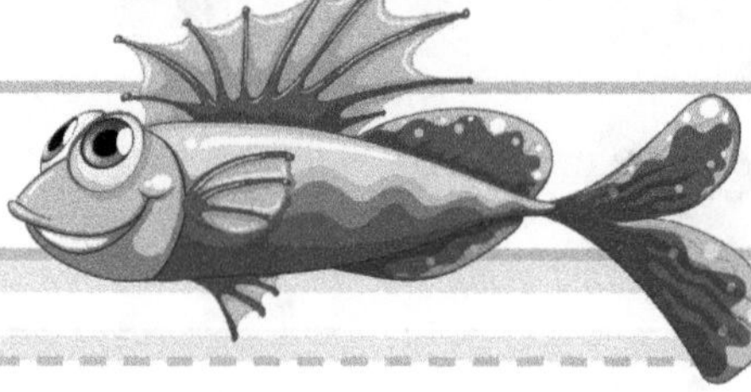

3. Draw an array for each. Write the multiplication statement.

a) 5 × 3

b) 4 × 6

c) 1 × 5

d) 2 × 7

e) 3 × 4

f) 6 × 2

g) 4 × 4

h) 6 × 1

i) 3 × 2

j) 7 × 4

k) 2 × 5

l) 5 × 5

Multiplying by Skip Counting

When you multiply two numbers, the answer is called the product.
Skip count on the number line to multiply. Write the product.

3 × 4 =

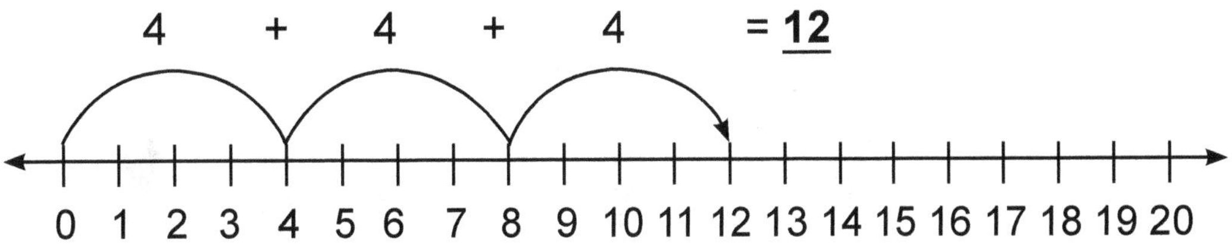
4 + 4 + 4 = 12
0 1 2 3 4 5 6 7 8 9 10 11 12 13 14 15 16 17 18 19 20

3 × 4 = **12**

4 × 5 =

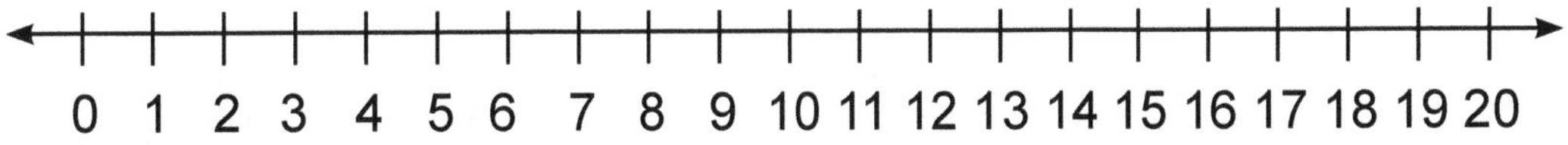
0 1 2 3 4 5 6 7 8 9 10 11 12 13 14 15 16 17 18 19 20

4 × 5 = ______

2 × 5 =

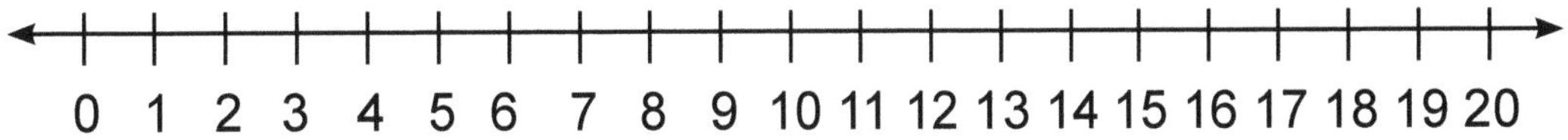
0 1 2 3 4 5 6 7 8 9 10 11 12 13 14 15 16 17 18 19 20

2 × 5 = ______

2 × 9 =

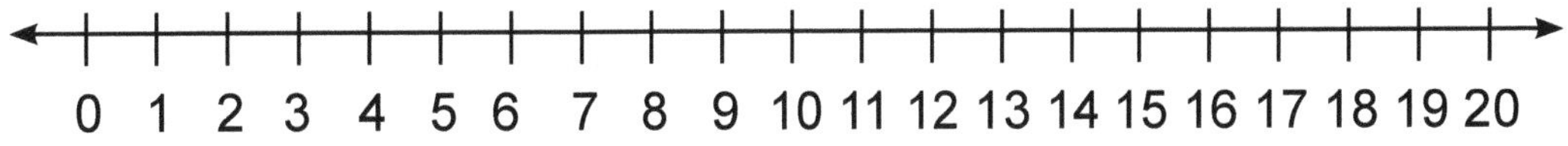
0 1 2 3 4 5 6 7 8 9 10 11 12 13 14 15 16 17 18 19 20

2 × 9 = ______

Skip Counting

Fill in the missing numbers.

1. Count by 3s.

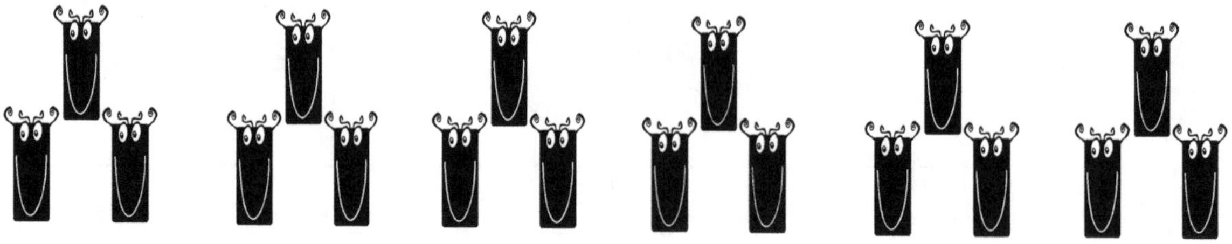

There are _________ groups of three creatures. There are _________ creatures altogether.

2 . Count by 5s.

There are _________ groups of five creatures. There are _________ creatures altogether.

3. Count by 10s.

There are _________ groups of ten creatures. There are _________ creatures altogether.

Addition and Multiplication

1. Write the addition sentence and the multiplication sentence.

Look at the groups of 3.

Addition Sentence	Multiplication Sentence
There are 3 equal groups.	There are 3 groups of 3.
3 + 3 + 3 = **9**	3 × 3 = **9**

6 + 6 = _____ 2 × 6 = _____

2 + 2 + 2 = _____ 3 × 2 = _____

10 + 10 = _____ 2 × 10 = _____

3 + 3 + 3 + 3 = _____ 4 × 3 = _____

7 + 7 = _____ 2 × 7 = _____

8 + 8 = _____ 2 × 8 = _____

Addition and Multiplication (continued)

2. Write the addition sentence and the multiplication sentence.

___ + ___ + ___ = ___ ___ × ___ = ___

___ + ___ = ___ ___ × ___ = ___

___ + ___ = ___ ___ × ___ = ___

___ + ___ + ___ + ___ + ___ = ___ ___ × ___ = ___

___ + ___ = ___ ___ × ___ = ___

___ + ___ + ___ + ___ = ___ ___ × ___ = ___

___ + ___ + ___ + ___ = ___ ___ × ___ = ___

___ + ___ = ___ ___ × ___ = ___

___ + ___ + ___ + ___ + ___ = ___ ___ × ___ = ___

Using Doubles to Multiply

What is the double of 13?

13 = 10 + 3
The double of 10 is 20.
The double of 3 is 6.
20 + 6 = 26
So, the double of 13 is 26.

1. Draw a model. Then find the double.

What is the double of 15?

15 = 10 + ___

The double of 10 is ___.

The double of ___ is ___.

___ + ___ = ___

So, the double of 15 is ___.

What is the double of 17?

17 = 10 + ___

The double of 10 is ___.

The double of ___ is ___.

___ + ___ = ___

So, the double of 17 is ____.

What is the double of 14?

14 = 10 + ___

The double of 10 is ___.

The double of ___ is ___.

___ + ___ = ___

So, the double of 14 is ___.

What is the double of 21?

21 = 20 + ___

The double of 20 is ___.

The double of ___ is ___.

___ + ___ = ___

So, the double of 21 is ___.

Using Doubles to Multiply (continued)

If you know 2 times a number, you can double to find 4 times the number.

2 × 6 = 12

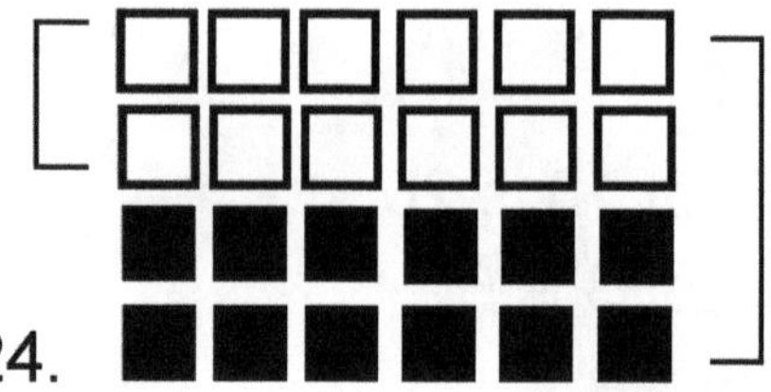

4 × 6 = 24

For 4 × 6, you know:

2 × 6 = 12

Double 2 to get 4. Double the product to get 24.

So, 4 × 6 = 24.

2. Use doubles to multiply. Draw an array to help.

a) 2 × 7 = ___

So, 4 × 7 = ____

b) 2 × 8 = ___

So, 4 × 8 = ___

c) 2 × 5 = ___

So, 4 × 5 = ___

d) 2 × 9 = ___

So, 4 × 9 = ___

e) 3 × 5 = ___

So, 6 × 5 = ___

f) 3 × 6 = ___

So, 6 × 6 = ___

Match-Up Fun

Write each sum and product. Then match the sum to the product.

4 + 4 = ______

6 + 6 + 6 = ______

2 + 2 + 2 + 2 + 2 + 2 + 2 + 2 + 2 + 2 = ______

2 + 2 + 2 = ______

1 + 1 = ______

9 + 9 = ______

3 + 3 + 3 + 3 = ______

10 + 10 + 10 + 10 + 10 + 10 + 10 = ______

2 + 2 = ______

8 + 8 = ______

9 + 9 + 9 + 9 + 9 + 9 + 9 + 9 + 9 = ______

3 + 3 = ______

2 + 2 + 2 + 2 = ______

7 + 7 = ______

5 + 5 + 5 + 5 + 5 + 5 = ______

2 × 8 = ______

6 × 5 = ______

3 × 2 = ______

4 × 3 = ______

7 × 10 = ______

3 × 6 = ______

10 × 2 = ______

2 × 1 = ______

2 × 3 = ______

2 × 4 = ______

4 × 2 = ______

2 × 2 = ______

2 × 7 = ______

9 × 9 = ______

2 × 9 = ______

Hint: The answer in addition is called the **sum**.
The answer in multiplication is called the **product**.

Multiplication Fun

Find the product.

6 rows of 6

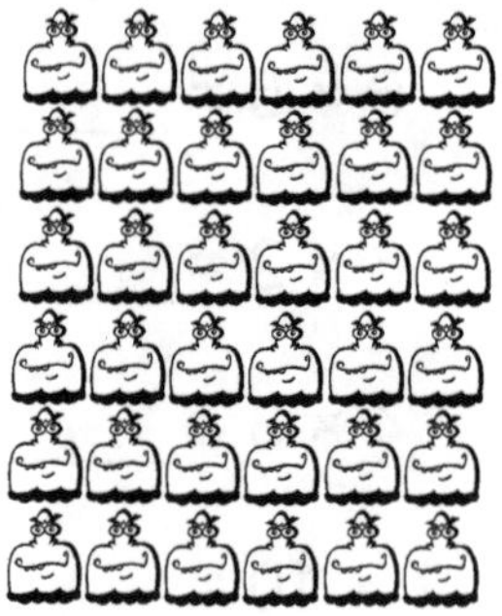

$6 \times 6 =$ ________

5 rows of 4

$5 \times 4 =$ ________

2 rows of 5

$2 \times 5 =$ ________

4 rows of 3

$4 \times 3 =$ ________

6 rows of 2

$6 \times 2 =$ ________

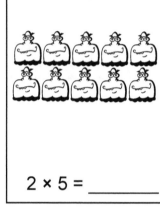

4 rows of 2

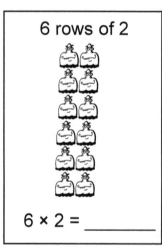

$4 \times 2 =$ ________

3 rows of 5

$3 \times 5 =$ ________

3 rows of 3

$3 \times 3 =$ ________

4 rows of 6

$4 \times 6 =$ ________

Multiplication Riddle

Why did the robot go back to school?

__ __ | __ __ __ | __ __ __ __ __ __ __
15 18 | 16 20 10 | 8 18 0 0 14 25 8

__ | __ __ __ __ __ __ | __ __ __ __ __ !
20 | 12 14 0 0 12 18 | 6 4 10 0 9

A 5 × 4 = ___	**E** 6 × 3 = ___	**G** 4 × 2 = ___	**H** 3 × 5 = ___
I 7 × 2 = ___	**L** 3 × 4 = ___	**N** 5 × 5 = ___	**R** 3 × 2 = ___
S 5 × 2 = ___	**T** 0 × 5 = ___	**U** 1 × 4 = ___	**W** 4 × 4 = ___
Y 3 × 3 = ___			

Watch out! Some letters are not used in the riddle.

Multiplying by 1, 2, and 3

Multiply.

6×3	1×3	9×1	2×1	4×2
5×2	5×3	1×2	8×2	9×3
3×2	4×1	0×2	2×3	3×1
0×3	5×1	2×2	6×1	7×2
3×3	6×2	8×3		

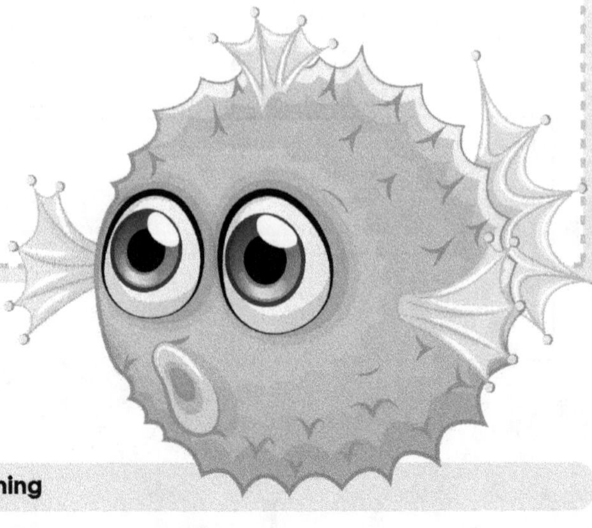

Doubles Plus One More Group

Find the double. Then add one more group.

3 × 4 =

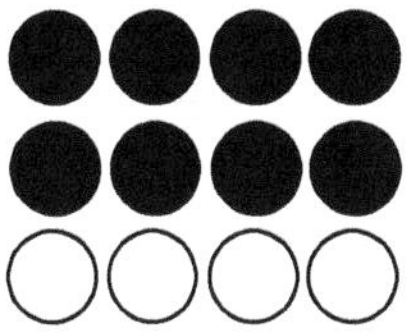

2 × 4 = 8

3 × 4 = **12**

The double of 4 is **8**.

One set is **4**.

8 + 4 = **12**.

So, 3 × 4 = **12**.

---

3 × 5 =

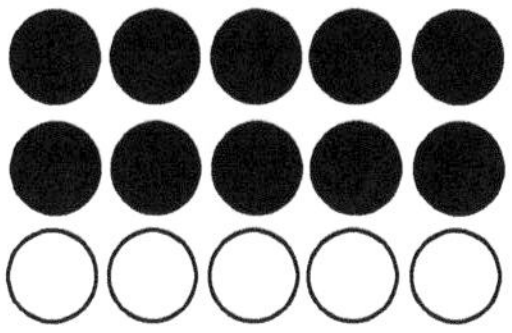

2 × 5 = ____

3 × 5 = ____

The double of 5 is ____.

One set is ____.

10 + ____ = ____.

So, 3 × 5 = ____.

---

3 × 7 =

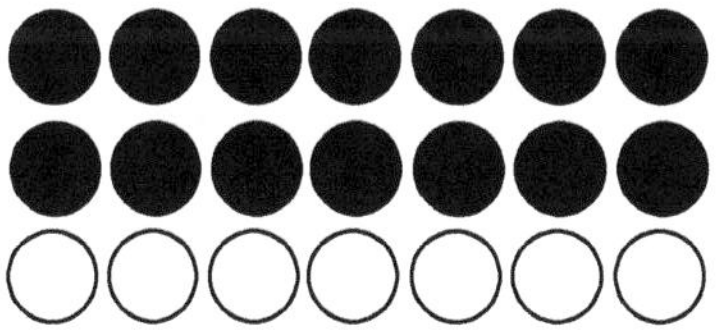

2 × 7 = ____

3 × 7 = ____

The double of 7 is ____.

One set is ____.

____ + ____ = ____.

So, 3 × 7 = ____.

---

3 × 6 =

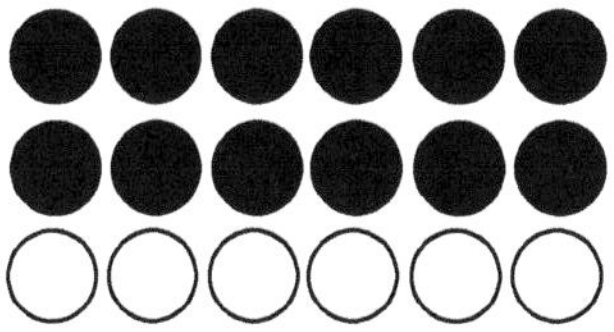

2 × 6 = ____

3 × 6 = ____

The double of 6 is ____.

One set is ____.

____ + ____ = ____.

So, 3 × 6 = ____.

Multiplying by 4, 5, and 6

Use an array to help find the product.

6 × 4 = ____	1 × 4 = ____	9 × 6 = ____	2 × 6 = ____	4 × 5 = ____
5 × 5 = ____	5 × 4 = ____	1 × 6 = ____	8 × 5 = ____	9 × 4 = ____
3 × 5 = ____	4 × 6 = ____	0 × 5 = ____	2 × 4 = ____	3 × 6 = ____
0 × 4 = ____	5 × 6 = ____	2 × 5 = ____	6 × 6 = ____	7 × 5 = ____

BRAIN STRETCH

Bessie made a family photo album. The photo album had 8 pages. Each page had 4 pictures. How many pictures were in the photo album altogether? Draw a picture to show how you know.

Multiplying by 7, 8, and 9

Use an array to help find the product.

6 × 9 = ____	1 × 9 = ____	9 × 7 = ____	2 × 7 = ____	4 × 8 = ____
5 × 8 = ____	5 × 9 = ____	1 × 7 = ____	8 × 8 = ____	9 × 9 = ____
3 × 8 = ____	4 × 7 = ____	0 × 8 = ____	2 × 9 = ____	3 × 7 = ____
0 × 9 = ____	5 × 7 = ____	2 × 8 = ____	6 × 7 = ____	7 × 7 = ____

BRAIN STRETCH

Bill had 8 book shelves. On each shelf there were 9 books. How many books were on the book shelves altogether? Draw a picture to show how you know.

Multiplying by 10

Use your favourite strategy to find the product.

1 × 10 = ____	9 × 10 = ____	2 × 10 = ____	6 × 10 = ____	4 × 10 = ____
5 × 10 = ____	3 × 10 = ____	7 × 10 = ____	10 × 10 = ____	8 × 10 = ____
9 × 10 = ____	2 × 10 = ____	5 × 10 = ____	6 × 10 = ____	1 × 10 = ____
0 × 10 = ____	7 × 10 = ____	4 × 10 = ____	3 × 10 = ____	10 × 10 = ____
1 × 10 = ____	2 × 10 = ____	6 × 10 = ____		

Math Joke

Solve to find the answer.

Why did David throw a clock out the window?

4 × 9 =	☐	A	6 × 5 =	☐	M
5 × 9 =	☐	D	6 × 2 =	☐	N
3 × 9 =	☐	E	10 × 10 =	☐	O
3 × 3 =	☐	F	8 × 8 =	☐	S
4 × 4 =	☐	H	2 × 4 =	☐	T
5 × 5 =	☐	I	10 × 7 =	☐	W
2 × 2 =	☐	L	8 × 5 =	☐	Y

Watch out! Some letters may not be used in the riddle.

__ __ | __ __ __ __ __ __ | __ __ | __ __ __

16 27 | 70 36 12 8 27 45 | 8 100 | 64 27 27

__ __ __ __ | __ __ __ !

8 25 30 27 | 9 4 40 !

BRAIN STRETCH

7	9	6	8
× ☐	× ☐	× ☐	× ☐
56	81	42	64

Introducing Division

Use a circle to divide into groups. Complete the division sentence.

1. Divide 10 creatures into groups of 2.

________ groups $10 \div 2 =$ ________

2. Divide 12 creatures into groups of 3.

________ groups $12 \div 3 =$ ________

3. Divide 8 creatures into groups of 2.

________ groups $8 \div 2 =$ ________

4. Divide 10 creatures into groups of 5.

________ groups $10 \div 5 =$ ________

5. Divide 12 creatures into groups of 3.

________ groups $12 \div 3 =$ ________

Dividing by Skip Counting

Skip count on the number line to divide. Write the answer.

18 ÷ 3 =

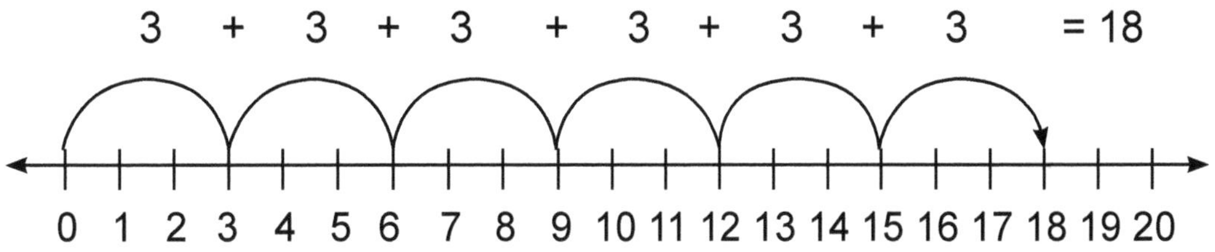
3 + 3 + 3 + 3 + 3 + 3 = 18
0 1 2 3 4 5 6 7 8 9 10 11 12 13 14 15 16 17 18 19 20

It takes **<u>6</u>** skips of 3 units to reach ___.   18 ÷ 3 = **<u>6</u>**

16 ÷ 2 =

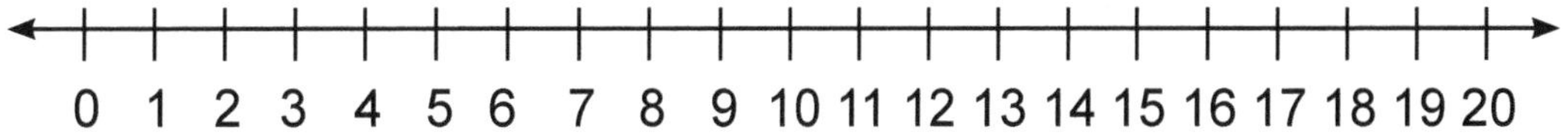
0 1 2 3 4 5 6 7 8 9 10 11 12 13 14 15 16 17 18 19 20

It takes ___ skips of 2 to reach ___.   16 ÷ 2 = ___

15 ÷ 5 =

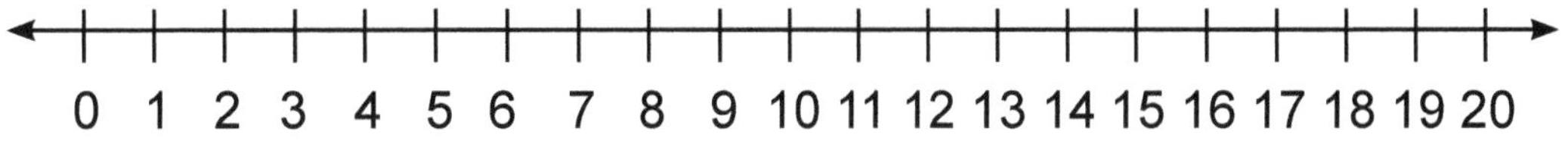
0 1 2 3 4 5 6 7 8 9 10 11 12 13 14 15 16 17 18 19 20

It takes ___ skips of ___ to reach ___.   15 ÷ 5 = ___

20 ÷ 4 =

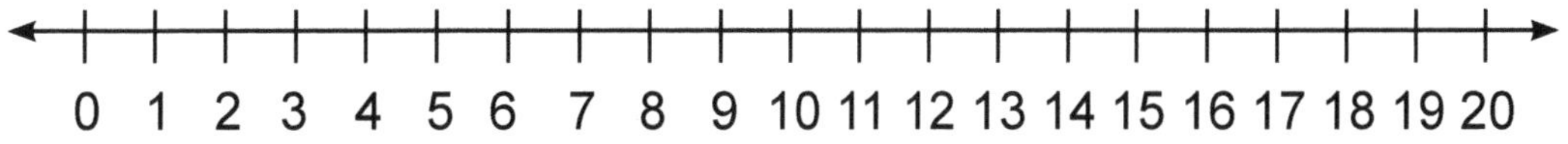
0 1 2 3 4 5 6 7 8 9 10 11 12 13 14 15 16 17 18 19 20

It takes ___ skips of ___ to reach ___.   20 ÷ 4 = ___

Division Fun

Write the division sentence.

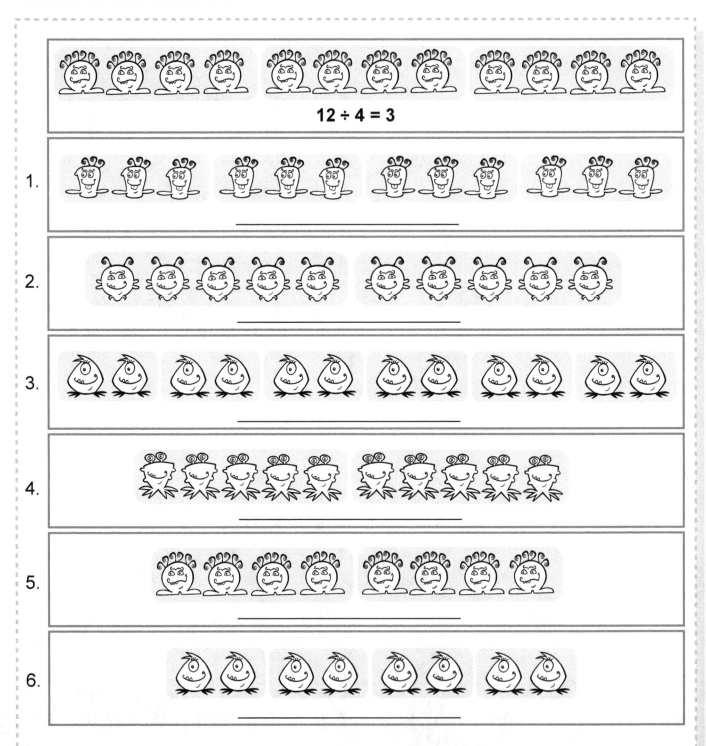

12 ÷ 4 = 3

1. 

____

2. 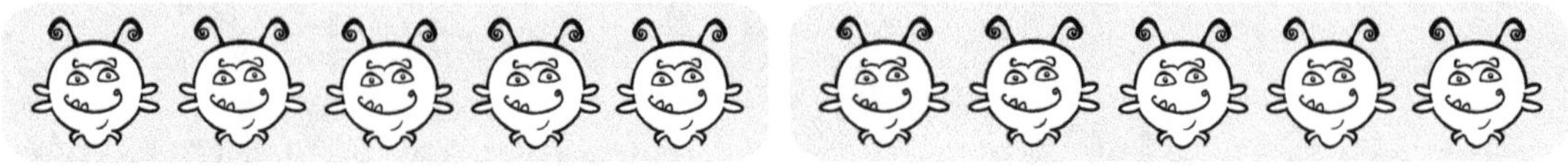

____

3. 

____

4. 

____

5. 

____

6. 

____

Division Riddle

What is a robot's favourite meal?

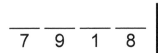

___ ___ ___ ___ | ___ ___ ___ | ___ ___ ___ ___ ___ !

7 9 1 8 | 2 7 3 | 6 5 4 1 8

A 10 ÷ 5 = ______	**B** 18 ÷ 3 = ______	**D** 12 ÷ 4 = ______	**L** 16 ÷ 4 = ______
N 28 ÷ 4 = ______	**O** 10 ÷ 2 = ______	**S** 16 ÷ 2 = ______	**T** 8 ÷ 8 = ______
U 9 ÷ 1 = ______			

Watch out! Some letters are not used in the riddle.

BRAIN STRETCH

Liam planted 40 trees. There are 8 trees in each row. How many rows of trees are there? Draw an array. Solve the problem.

Relating Addition and Division

Fill in the missing numbers.

1. 4 + 4 + 4 = ______ ______ ÷ 4 = 3
   ______ groups of the number ______

2. 3 + 3 + 3 + 3 + 3 + 3 + 3 + 3 + 3 = ______ ______ ÷ 3 = 9
   ______ groups of the number ______

3. 10 + 10 + 10 + 10 + 10 = ______ ______ ÷ 10 = 5
   ______ groups of the number ______

4. 5 + 5 = ______ 10 ÷ ______ = 2
   ______ groups of the number ______

5. 6 + 6 + 6 + 6 = ______ ______ ÷ 6 = 4
   ______ groups of the number ______

6. 4 + 4 + 4 + 4 + 4 + 4 + 4 + 4 = ______ 32 ÷ 4 = ______
   ______ groups of the number ______

7. 5 + 5 + 5 + 5 + 5 + 5 = ______ ______ ÷ 5 = 6
   ______ groups of the number ______

8. 2 + 2 + 2 + 2 + 2 + 2 + 2 + 2 = ______ 16 ÷ ______ = 8
   ______ groups of the number ______

9. 5 + 5 + 5 + 5 + 5 + 5 + 5 + 5 = ______ 40 ÷ 8 = ______
   ______ groups of the number ______

10. 4 + 4 + 4 + 4 + 4 = ______ 20 ÷ 4 = ______
    ______ groups of the number ______

Related Facts

Fill in the missing number.

5 × 6 = 30 30 ÷ 6 = ________	2 × 2 = 4 4 ÷ 2 = ________	3 × 5 = 15 15 ÷ 5 = ________
1 × 3 = 3 3 ÷ 3 = ________	5 × 4 = 20 20 ÷ 4 = ________	2 × 6 = 12 12 ÷ 6 = ________
4 × 1 = 4 4 ÷ 4 = ________	4 × 8 = 32 32 ÷ 8 = ________	3 × ________ = 3 3 ÷ 1 = 3
5 × 5 = 25 25 ÷ ________ = 5	3 × 4 = 12 ________ ÷ 4 = 3	4 × 7 = 28 28 ÷ ________ = 4
4 × 5 = 20 20 ÷ 5 = ________	3 × 6 = 18 18 ÷ 6 = ________	
2 × 9 = ________ 18 ÷ 2 = 9	10 × 4 = 40 ________ ÷ 10 = 4	

Dividing by 1, 2, and 3

Divide.

$1\overline{)6}$	$3\overline{)3}$	$1\overline{)7}$	$1\overline{)4}$	$2\overline{)12}$
$1\overline{)5}$	$3\overline{)21}$	$2\overline{)2}$	$1\overline{)1}$	$2\overline{)4}$
$2\overline{)10}$	$1\overline{)2}$	$2\overline{)18}$	$3\overline{)9}$	$1\overline{)3}$
$3\overline{)6}$	$1\overline{)9}$	$3\overline{)27}$	$1\overline{)8}$	$3\overline{)24}$
$3\overline{)15}$	$2\overline{)16}$	$3\overline{)18}$	$3\overline{)12}$	$2\overline{)10}$

Dividing by 4, 5, and 6

Divide.

$6\overline{)60}$	$6\overline{)54}$	$4\overline{)32}$	$4\overline{)16}$	$5\overline{)25}$
$5\overline{)35}$	$6\overline{)36}$	$4\overline{)4}$	$5\overline{)45}$	$6\overline{)30}$
$5\overline{)40}$	$4\overline{)12}$	$5\overline{)50}$	$6\overline{)12}$	$4\overline{)20}$
$6\overline{)48}$	$4\overline{)24}$	$5\overline{)20}$	$4\overline{)8}$	$5\overline{)10}$
$6\overline{)18}$	$6\overline{)42}$	$4\overline{)28}$	$5\overline{)10}$	$6\overline{)24}$

Dividing by 7, 8, and 9

Divide.

$9\overline{)81}$	$9\overline{)18}$	$8\overline{)40}$	$8\overline{)56}$	$7\overline{)70}$
$7\overline{)14}$	$9\overline{)36}$	$8\overline{)64}$	$7\overline{)49}$	$9\overline{)63}$
$7\overline{)35}$	$8\overline{)16}$	$7\overline{)21}$	$8\overline{)48}$	$7\overline{)28}$
$8\overline{)72}$	$7\overline{)56}$	$9\overline{)54}$	$8\overline{)8}$	$7\overline{)63}$
$9\overline{)45}$	$8\overline{)24}$	$9\overline{)9}$	$9\overline{)18}$	$8\overline{)32}$

Dividing by 10

Divide.

$10\overline{)80}$	$10\overline{)60}$	$10\overline{)10}$	$10\overline{)40}$	$10\overline{)20}$
$10\overline{)50}$	$10\overline{)100}$	$10\overline{)90}$	$10\overline{)10}$	$10\overline{)70}$
$10\overline{)20}$	$10\overline{)60}$	$10\overline{)30}$	$10\overline{)40}$	$10\overline{)20}$
$10\overline{)80}$	$10\overline{)70}$	$10\overline{)100}$	$10\overline{)50}$	$10\overline{)90}$

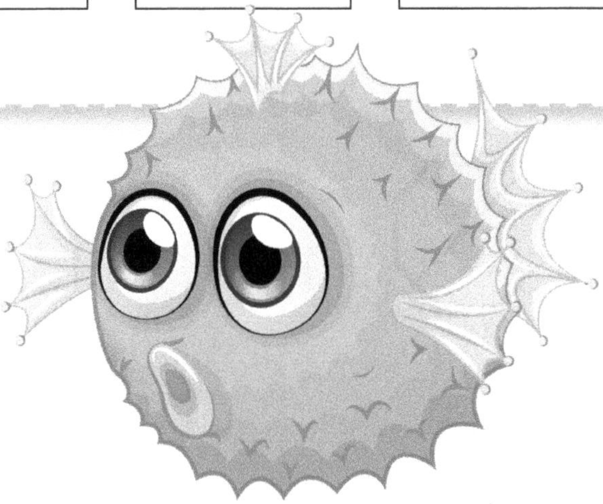

Fractions: Equal Parts

There are three equal parts.
Each part is one third.

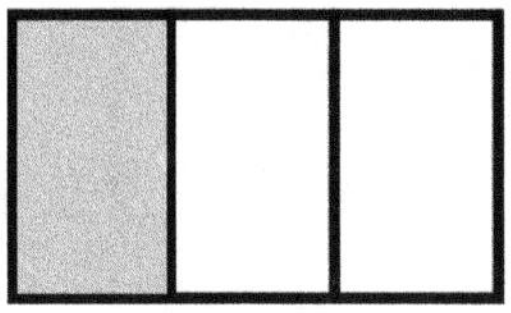

$\frac{1}{3}$ means that 1 out of 3 equal parts is shaded.

Shade one part of each shape. Write the fraction.

1. 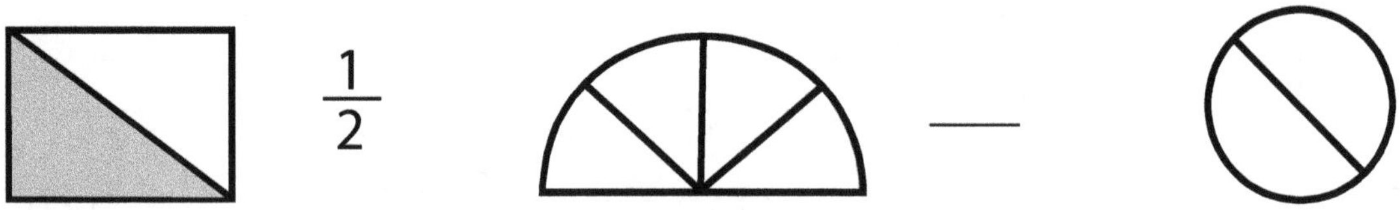

$\frac{1}{2}$ ___ ___

2. 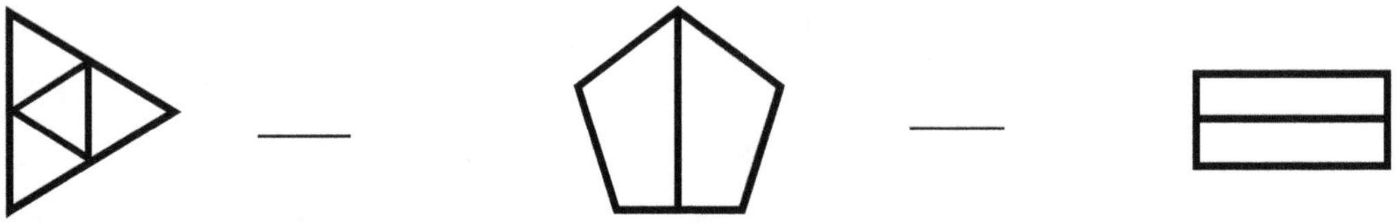

___ ___ ___

3. 

___ ___ ___

4. 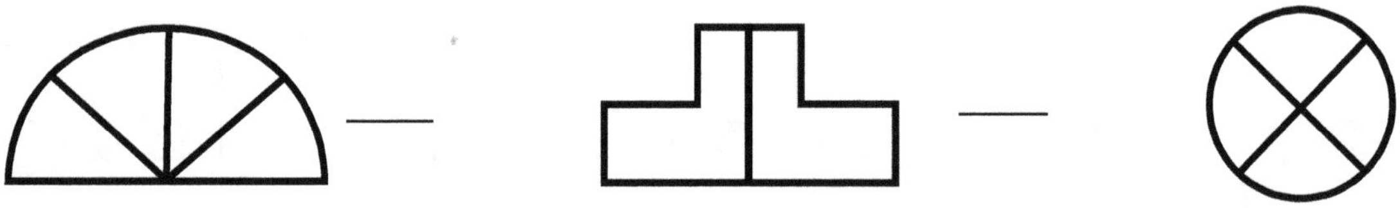

___ ___ ___

5. 

___ ___ ___

6. 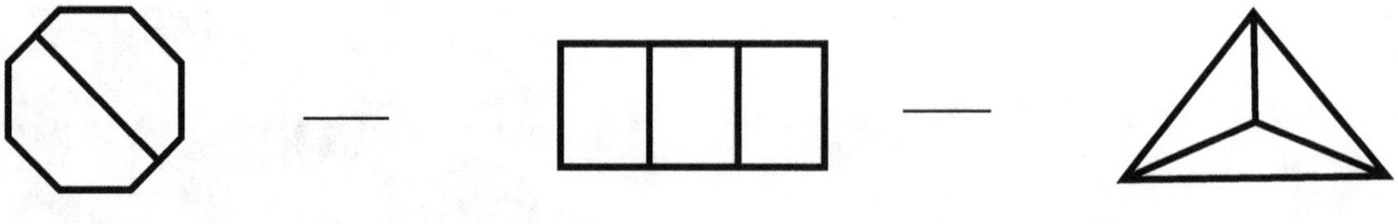

___ ___ ___

Exploring Fractions

Fractions show equal parts of a whole.
This means 3 out of 4 parts are shaded.

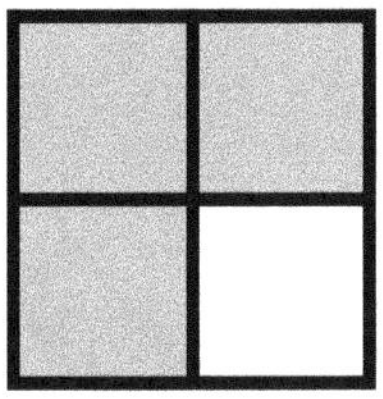

$\frac{3}{4}$ — 3: how many parts; 4: total parts

1. Write the fraction for each shaded part.

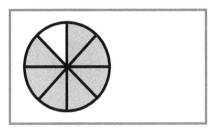

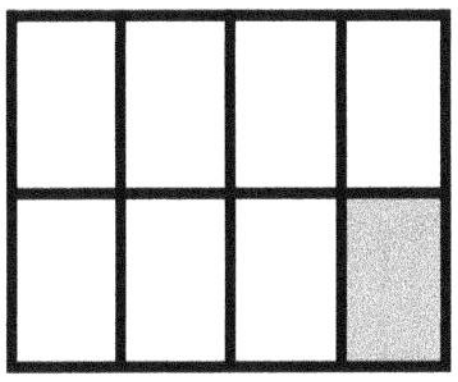

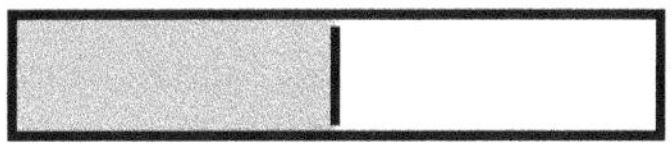

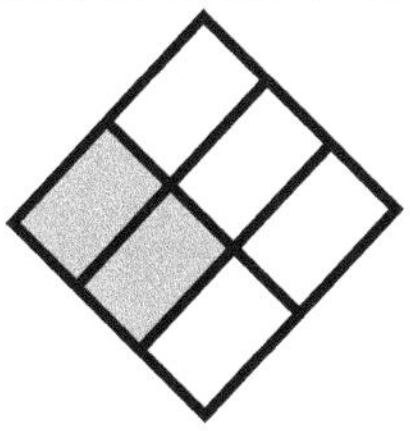

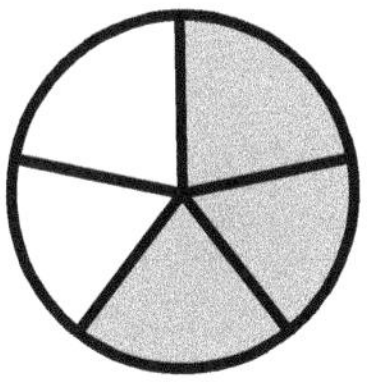

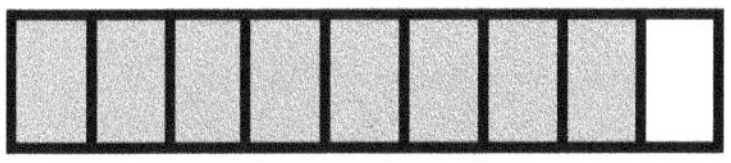

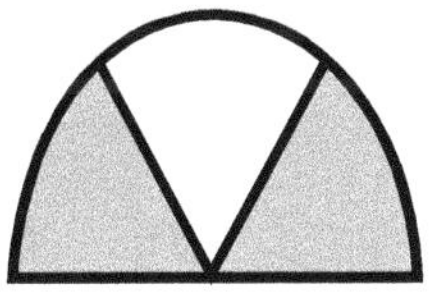

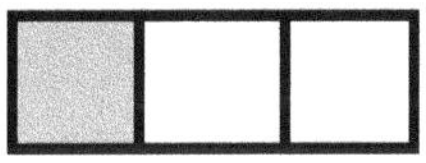

BRAIN STRETCH

Mixed numbers have a whole number part and a fraction part.
Choose the correct mixed number for the parts that are shaded.

1. 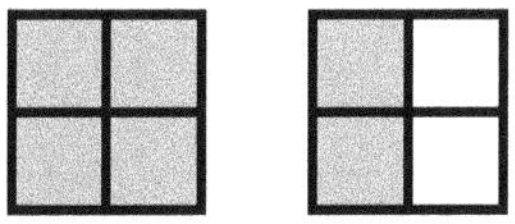

a) $\frac{4}{8}$ b) $\frac{4}{6}$ c) $1\frac{2}{4}$

2. 

a) $6\frac{2}{3}$ b) $\frac{3}{4}$ c) $3\frac{1}{2}$

Exploring Fractions (continued)

2. Write a fraction to show how much of the shape is not shaded.

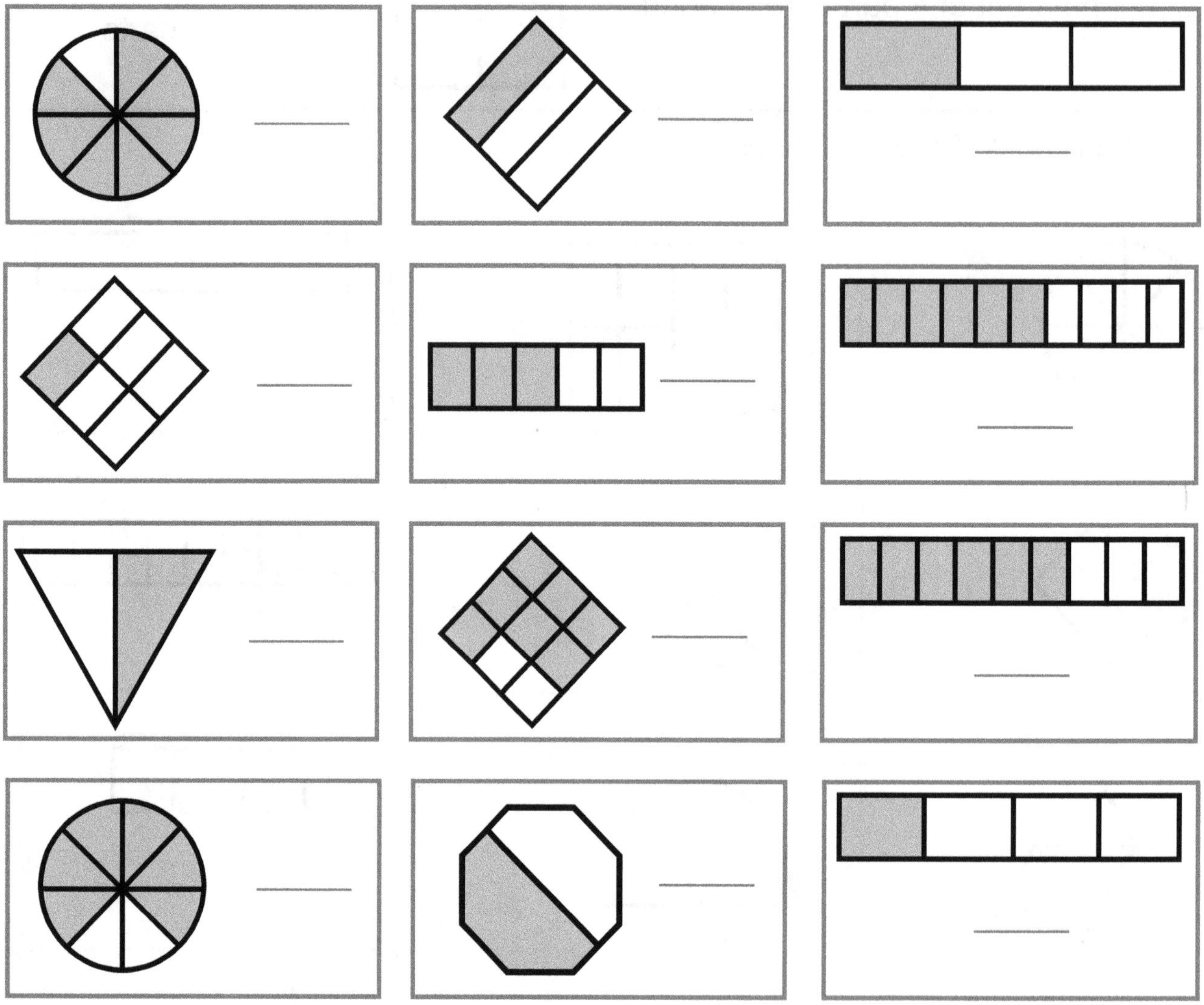

BRAIN STRETCH

a) Jane has 8 red beads and 3 blue beads. What fraction of Jane's beads are blue?

b) Tony has 3 oranges and 2 apples. What is the fraction of apples?

Colouring Fractions

Colour the fractions.

Colour $\frac{1}{4}$ blue.
Colour $\frac{3}{4}$ green.

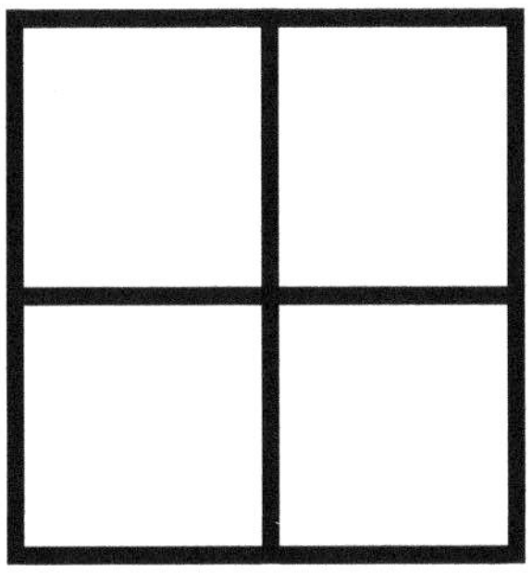

Colour $\frac{1}{2}$ blue.
Colour $\frac{1}{2}$ green.

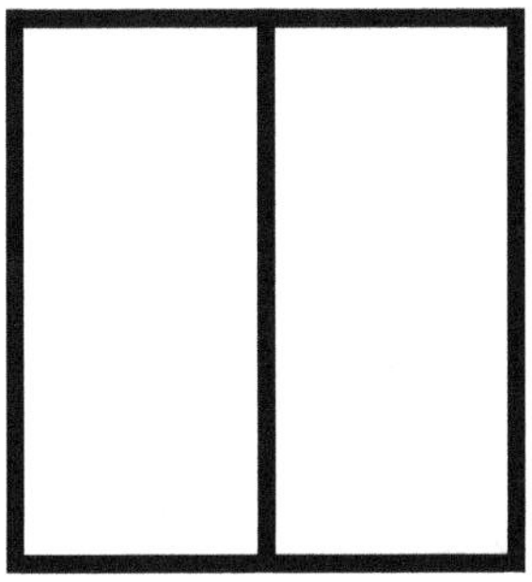

Colour $\frac{1}{4}$ blue.
Colour $\frac{1}{4}$ green.
Colour $\frac{2}{4}$ red.

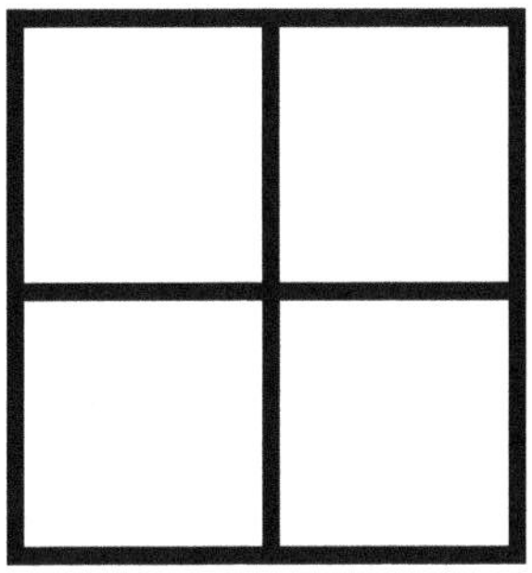

Colour $\frac{1}{2}$ blue.
Colour $\frac{1}{2}$ green.

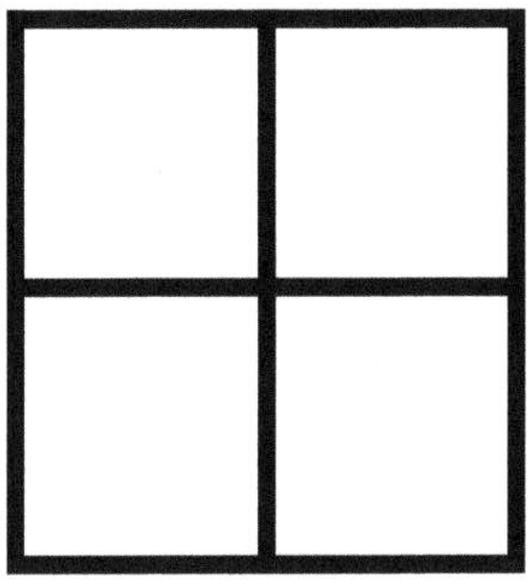

Colour $\frac{1}{3}$ blue.
Colour $\frac{2}{3}$ green.

Colour $\frac{1}{3}$ blue.
Colour $\frac{1}{3}$ green.
Colour $\frac{1}{3}$ red.

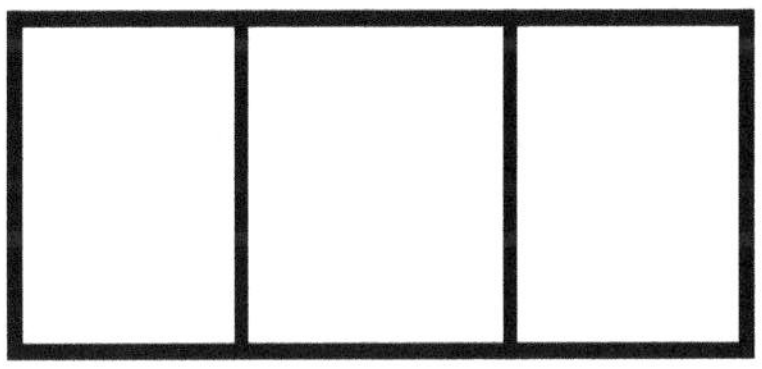

BRAIN STRETCH

Colour your own fractions. Name the fractions.

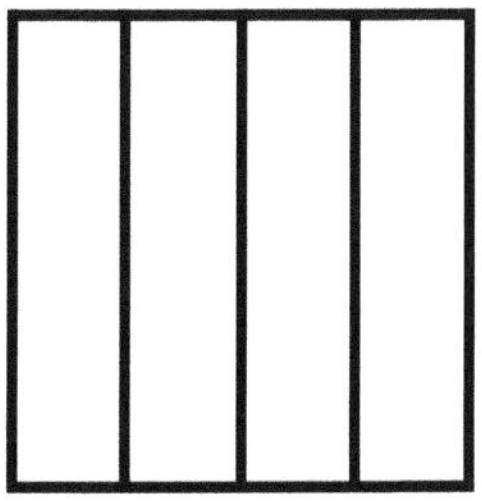 ___

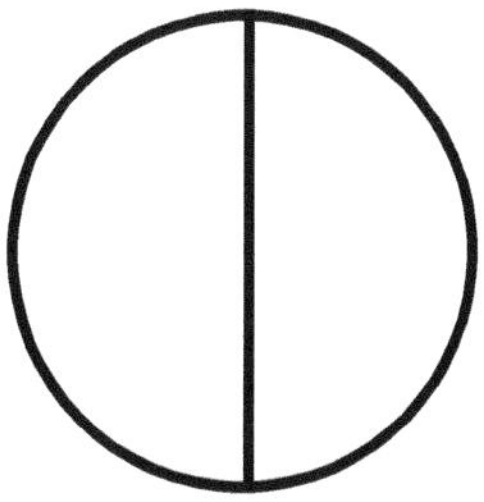 ___

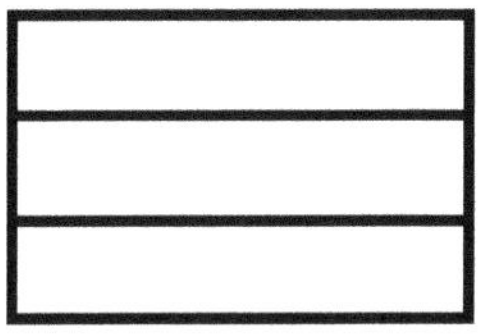 ___

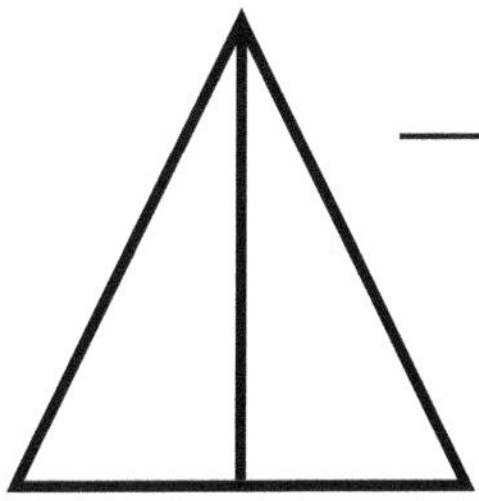 ___

Fractions as Part of a Group

Colour the fraction.

Colour $\frac{1}{4}$.

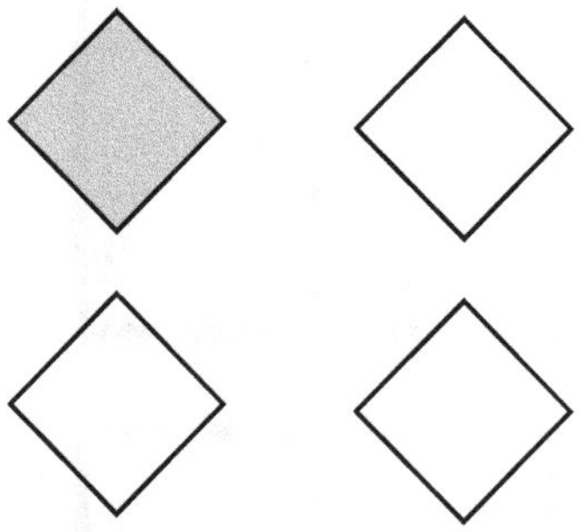

Colour $\frac{1}{3}$.

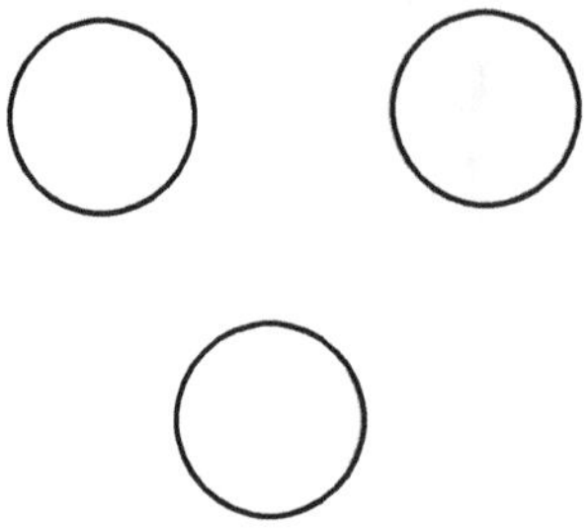

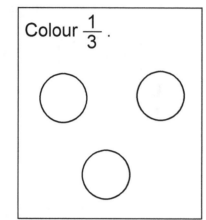

Colour $\frac{2}{4}$.

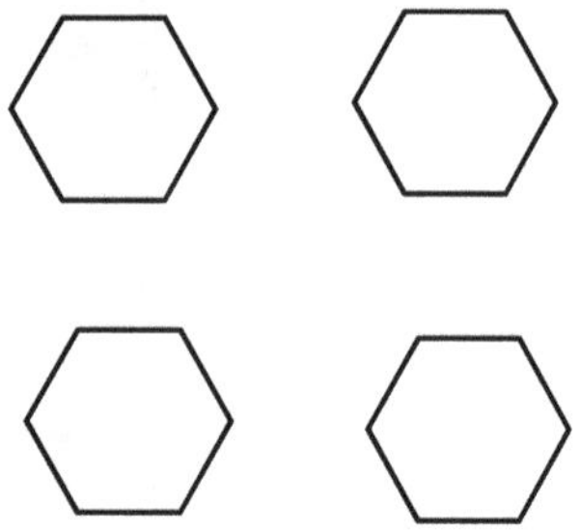

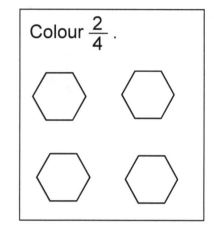

Colour $\frac{2}{3}$.

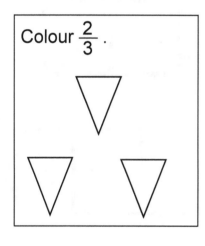

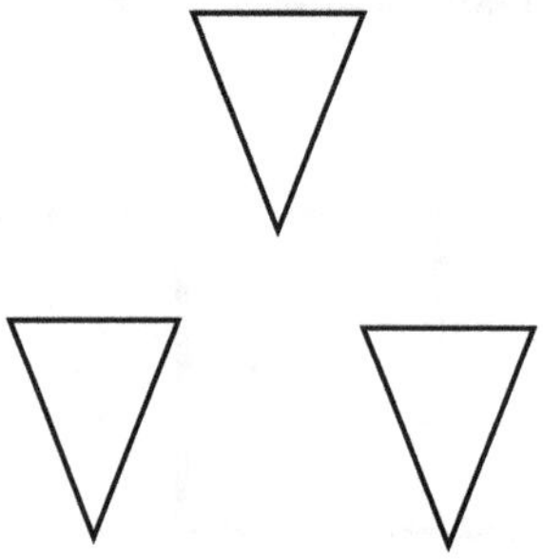

Colour $\frac{1}{2}$.

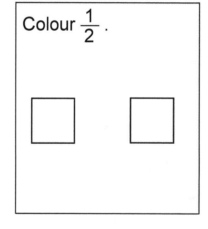

Colour $\frac{3}{4}$.

Colour $\frac{1}{2}$.

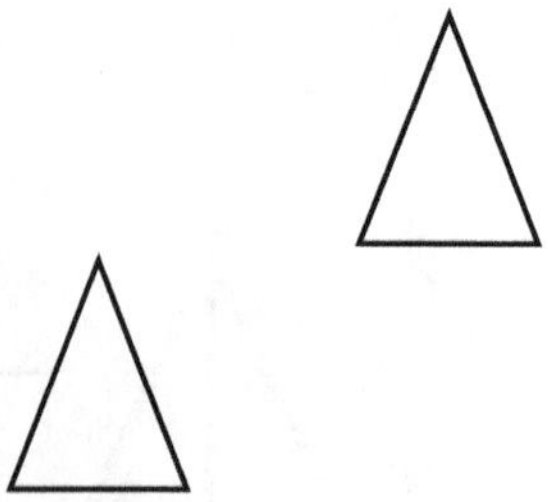

Colour $\frac{1}{3}$.

Colour $\frac{1}{2}$.

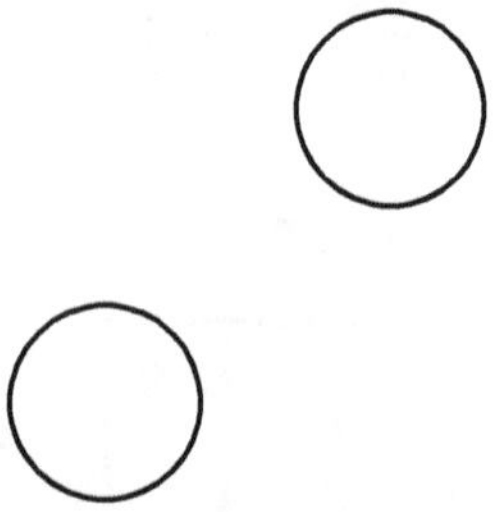

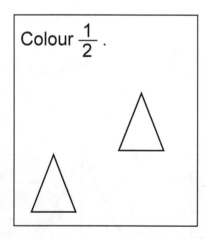

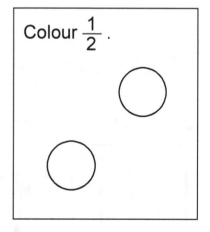

Fraction Problems

Draw a picture and show the answer as a fraction.

1. Nathan cut a pizza into 4 equal slices. He ate 2 slices.
   What fraction of the pizza did he eat?

______

2. Sue counts 8 mailboxes on her street. 3 are red.
   What fraction of the mailboxes are red?

______

3. Mia has 3 books from the library. She read 1 of them.
   What fraction of the books did she read?

______

4. Liz has 8 crackers for snack. She put cheese on
   2 of them. What fraction of the crackers have cheese?

______

5. Douglas has 2 cookies. He gave 1 cookie to his friend.
   What fraction of the cookies did he give away?

______

Exploring Polygons

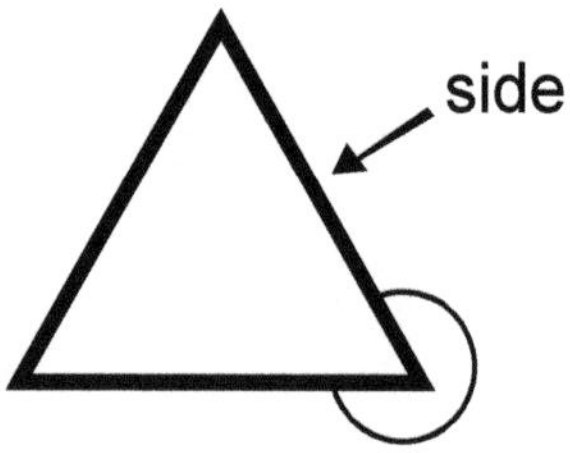
side

A polygon is a 2D shape with at least 3 sides.
A regular polygon has all sides equal and all angles equal.

A corner of a polygon is a vertex.
The plural is vertices.

1. Fill in the chart.

Shape	Trace the Shape	Number of Sides	Number of Vertices
triangle			
square			
pentagon			
hexagon			
octagon			

Exploring Polygons (continued)

2. Fill in the chart.

Shape	Trace the Shape	Number of Sides	Number of Vertices
rectangle			
rhombus			
parallelogram			
trapezoid			

BRAIN STRETCH

An irregular polygon does **not** have all sides equal and all angles equal. Draw two irregular polygons.

Exploring Polygons (continued)

3. Put an X if it is **not** a polygon. Colour the regular polygons blue.
Colour the irregular polygons red.

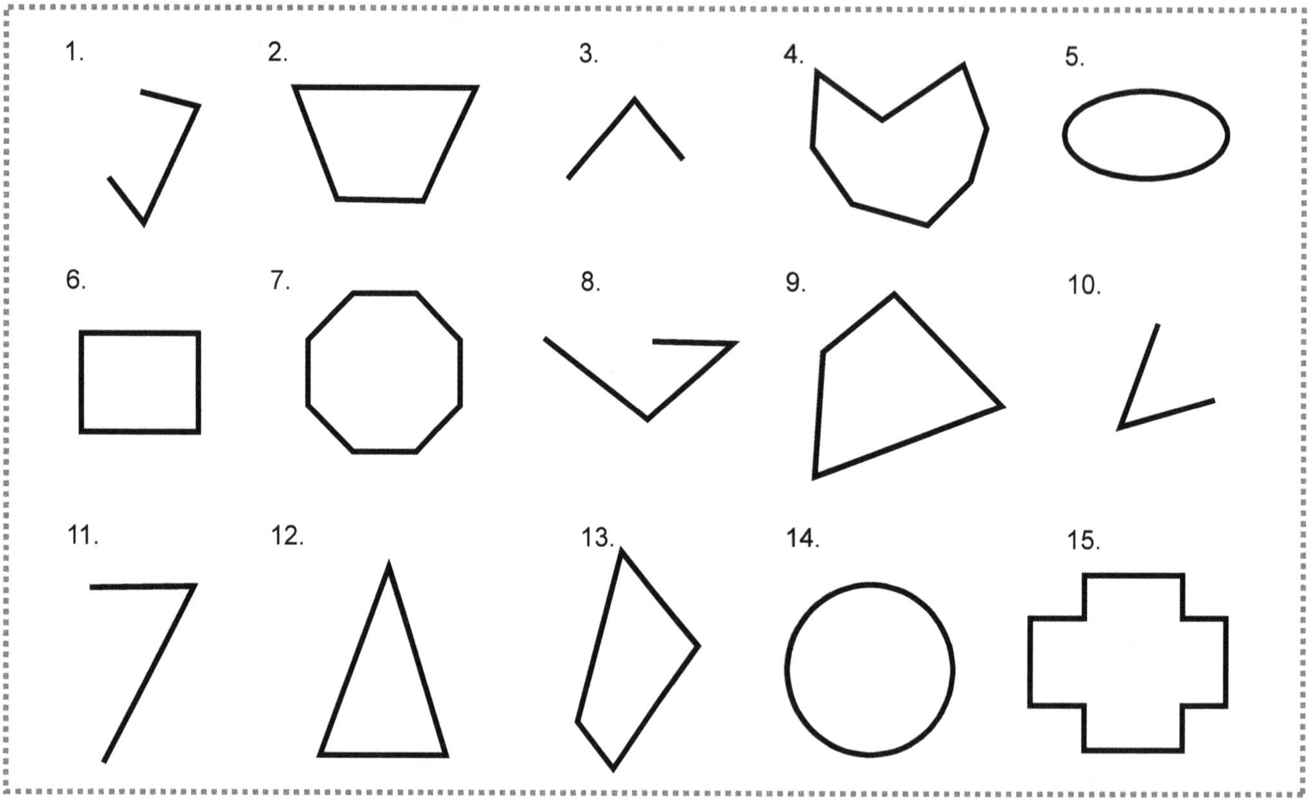
1.
2.
3.
4.
5.
6.
7.
8.
9.
10.
11.
12.
13.
14.
15.

BRAIN STRETCH

Quadrilaterals are polygons with 4 sides.
Colour the quadrilaterals orange. Put an X if it is **not** a quadrilateral.

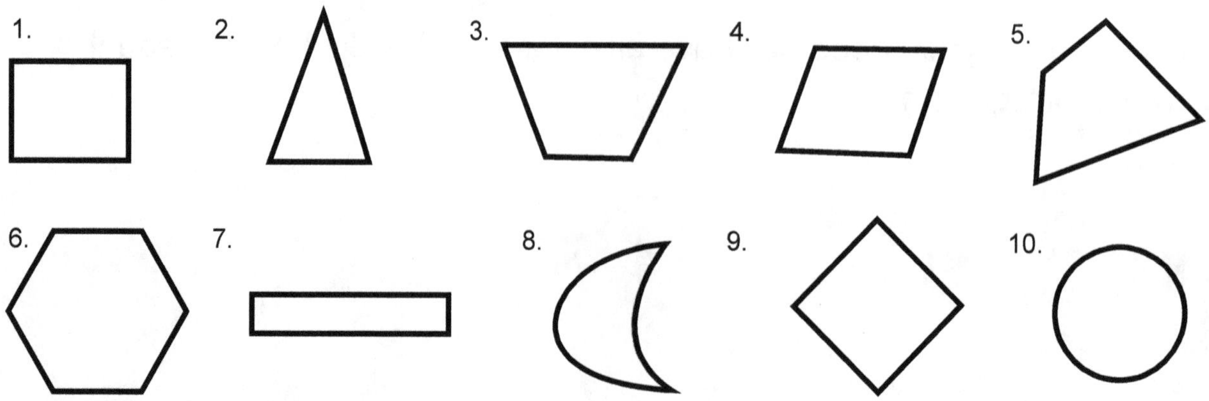
1.
2.
3.
4.
5.
6.
7.
8.
9.
10.

2D Shapes

Use the word box and write the correct name for each 2D shape.

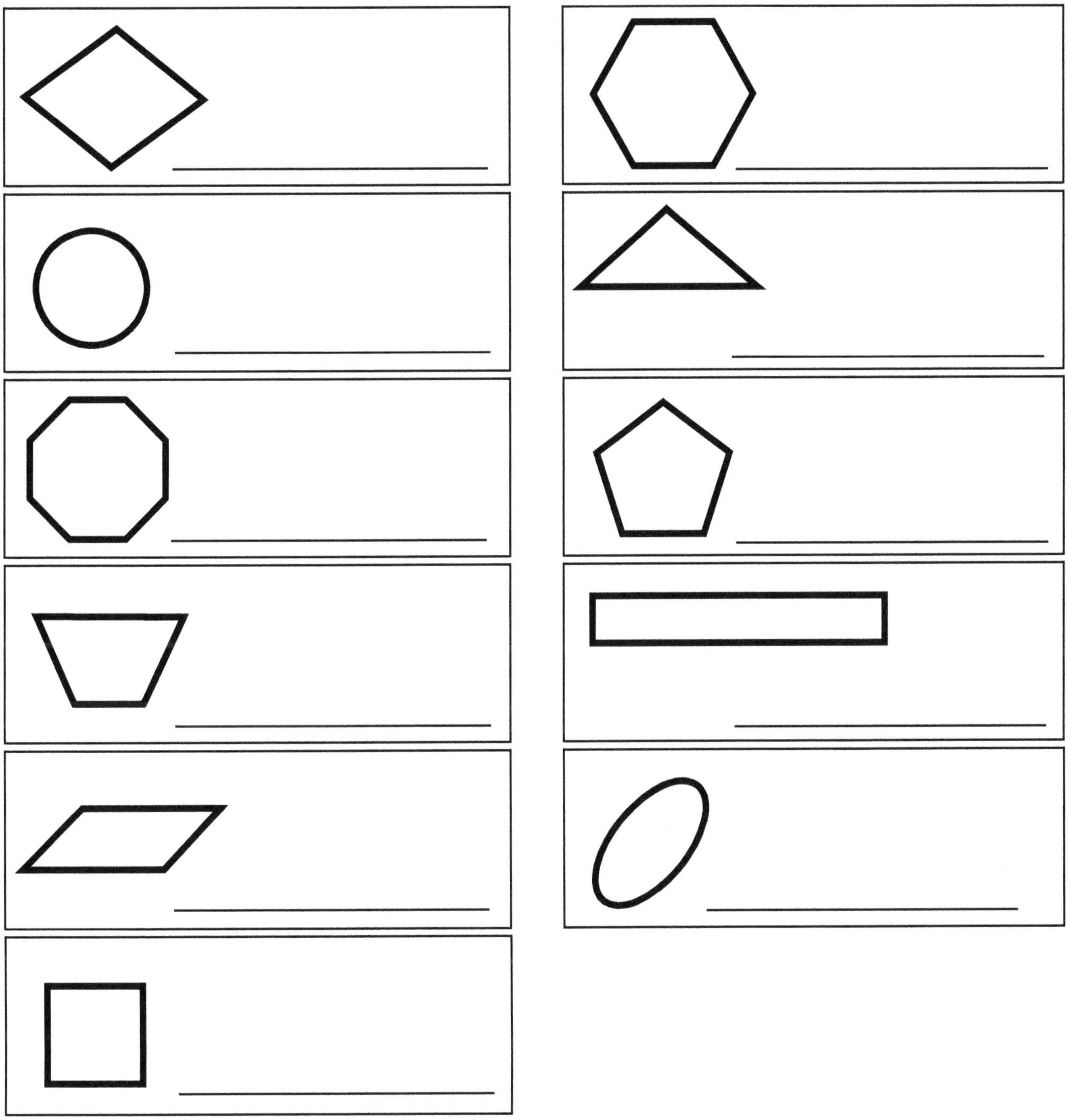

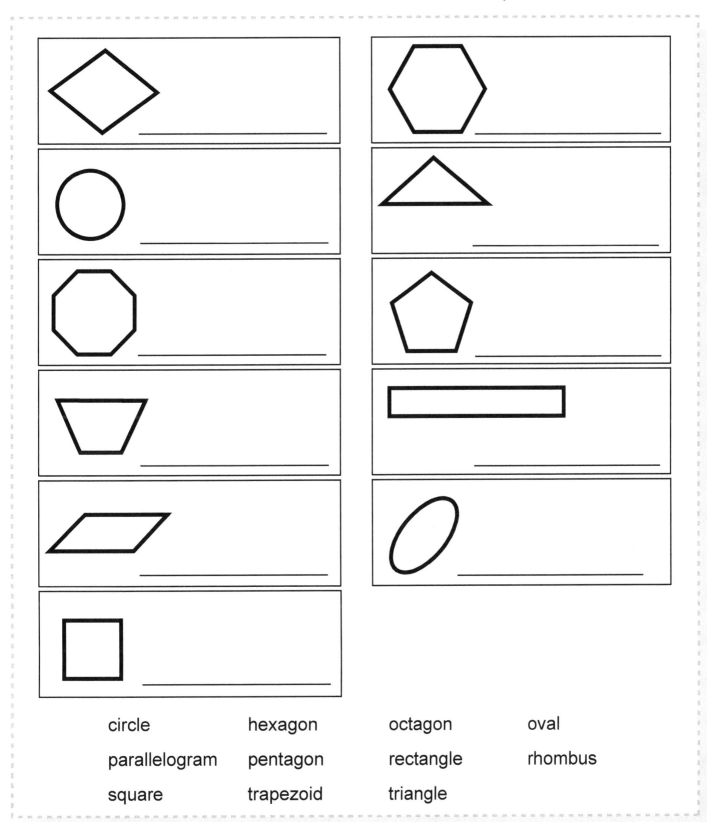

circle	hexagon	octagon	oval
parallelogram	pentagon	rectangle	rhombus
square	trapezoid	triangle	

Sorting 2D Shapes

Read the rule. Colour the shapes that follow the rule.

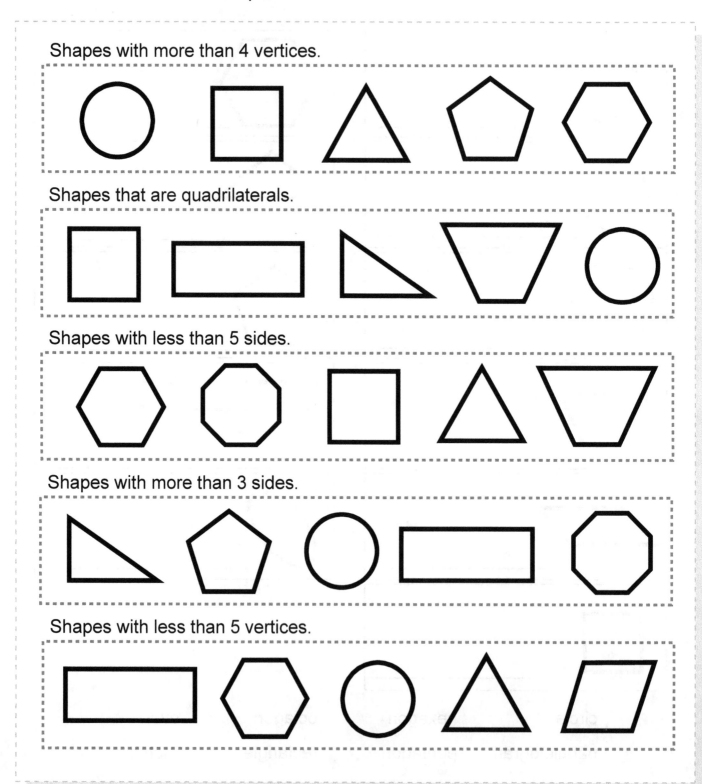

Shapes with more than 4 vertices.

Shapes that are quadrilaterals.

Shapes with less than 5 sides.

Shapes with more than 3 sides.

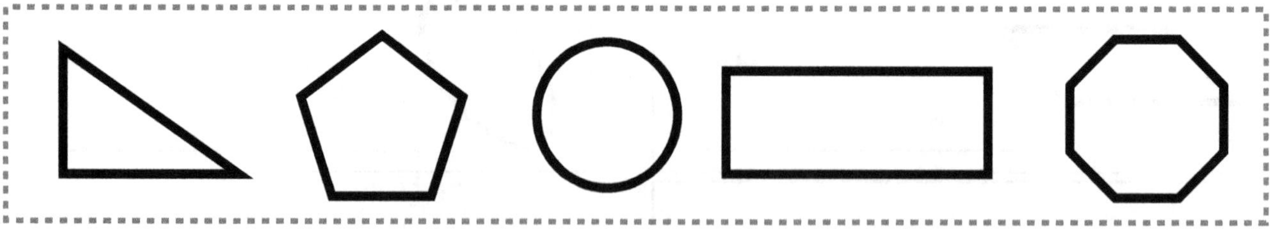

Shapes with less than 5 vertices.

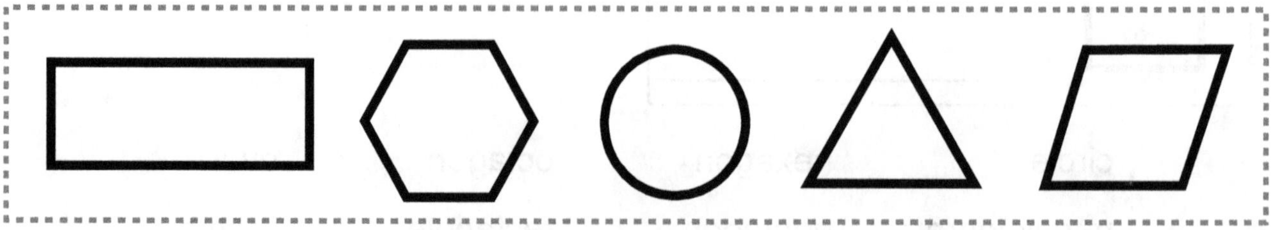

2D Shapes

Sort the 2D shapes into groups.

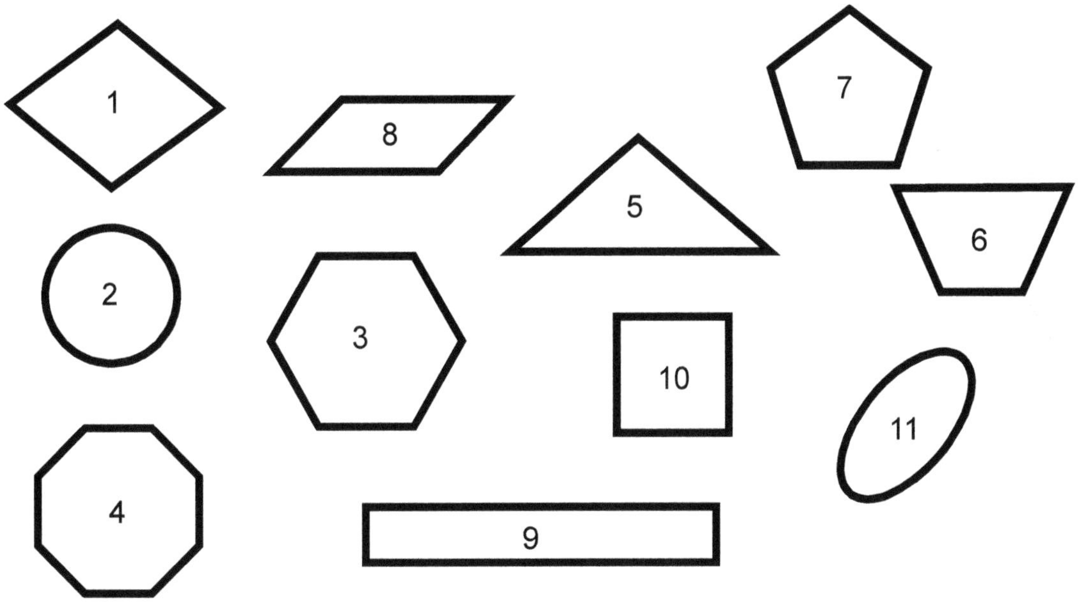
1
8
7
5
6
2
3
10
11
4
9

2D Shapes	Sorting Rule
	polygons that have only 3 sides
	polygons that have more than 5 sides
	polygons that have 4 vertices
	polygons that have square corners
	polygons that have more than 1 set of parallel lines

Identifying 3D Objects

1. Match the 3D object with its name.

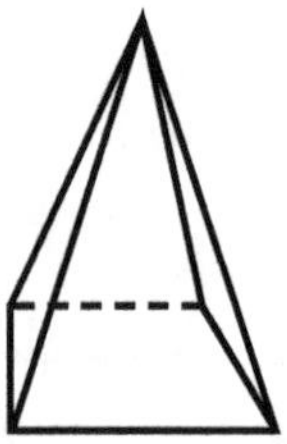

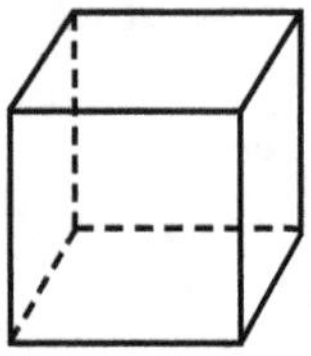

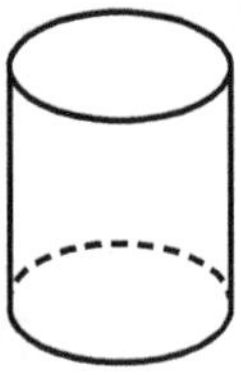

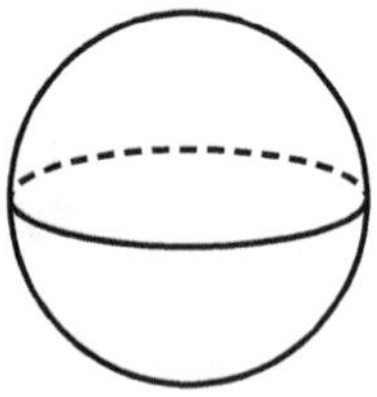

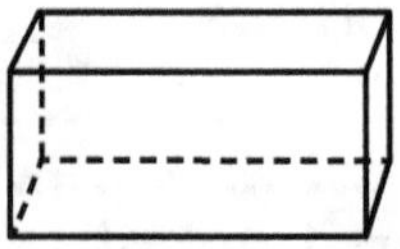

pyramid

cylinder

sphere

rectangular prism

cone

cube

Identifying 3D Objects (continued)

2. Match the name of the 3D object to an item it looks like. Circle the answer.

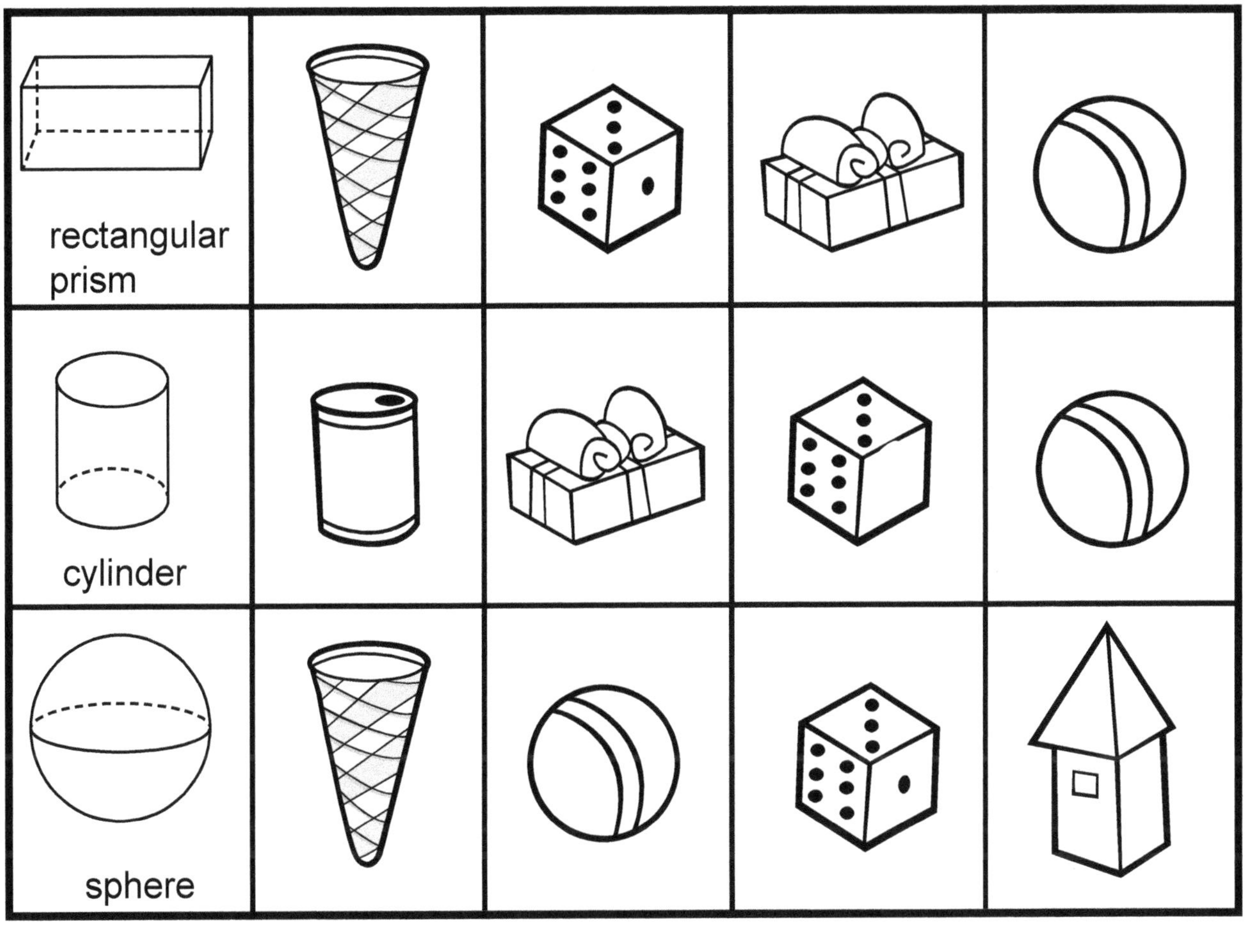
rectangular prism
cylinder
sphere

BRAIN STRETCH

Circle the 3D object that can be made from the pieces.

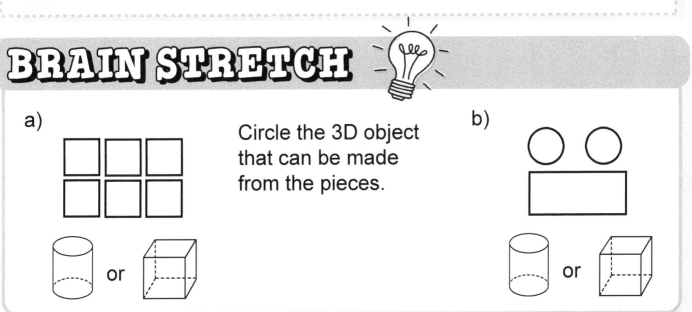

a)

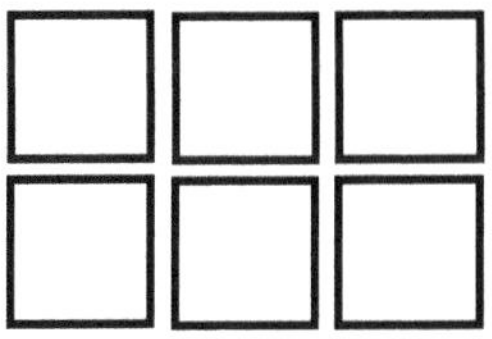

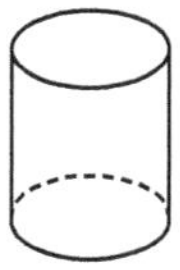 or 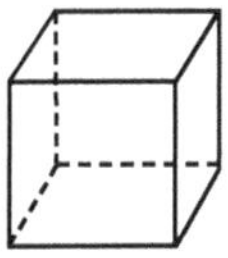

b)

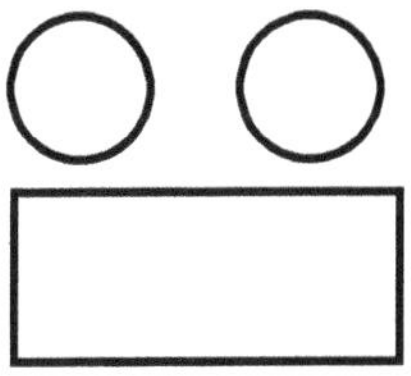

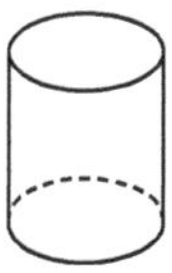 or 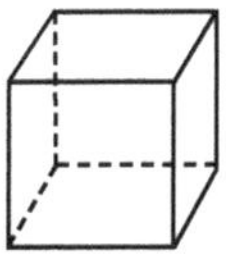

Attributes of 3D Objects

Complete the attribute chart.

3D Object	Name of Object	Number of Faces	Number of Edges	Number of Vertices
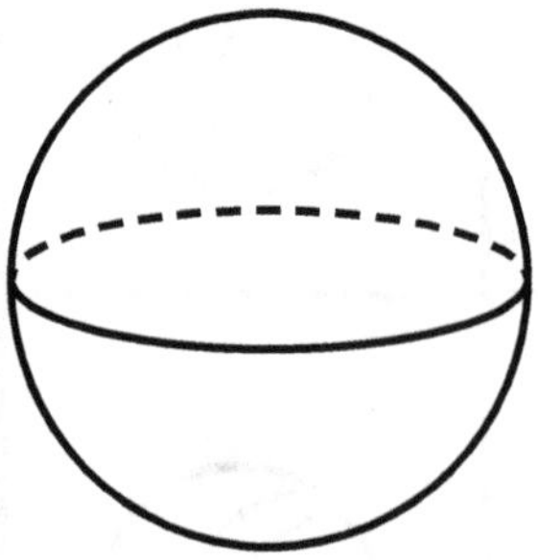				
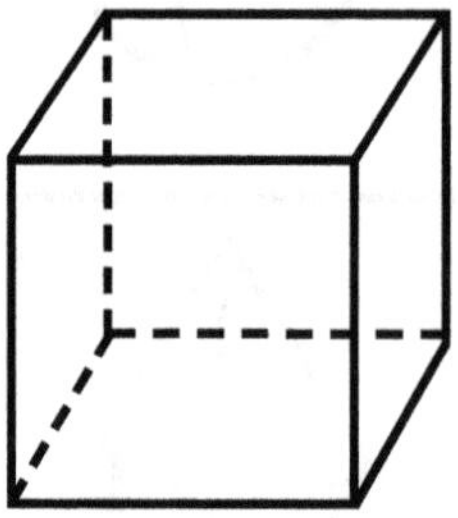				
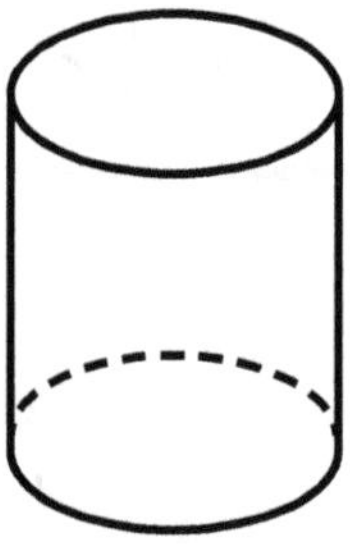				
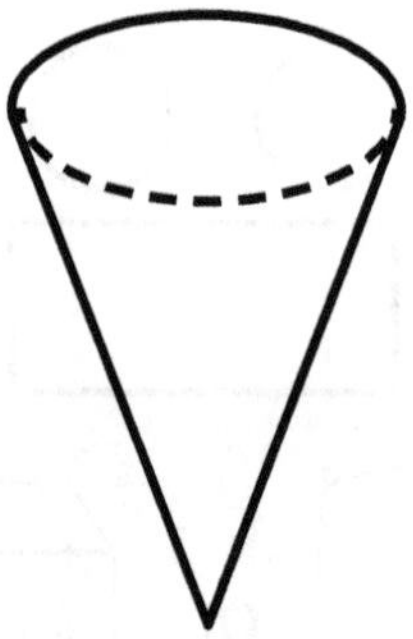				

3D Objects

Circle the name of the 3D object that you can make from the pieces.

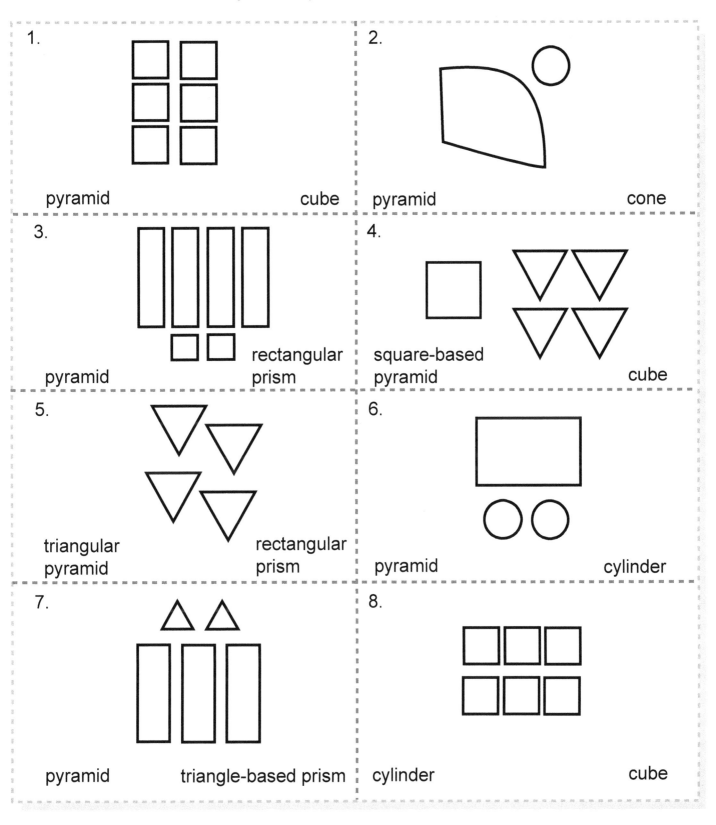

1.

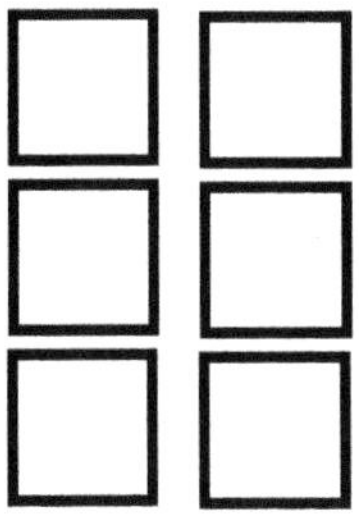

pyramid cube

2.

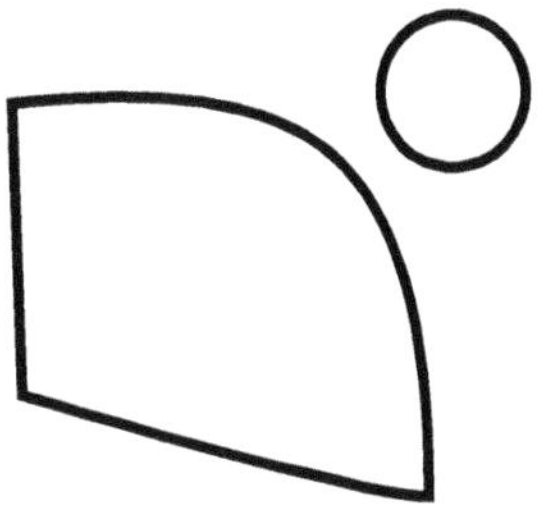

pyramid cone

3.

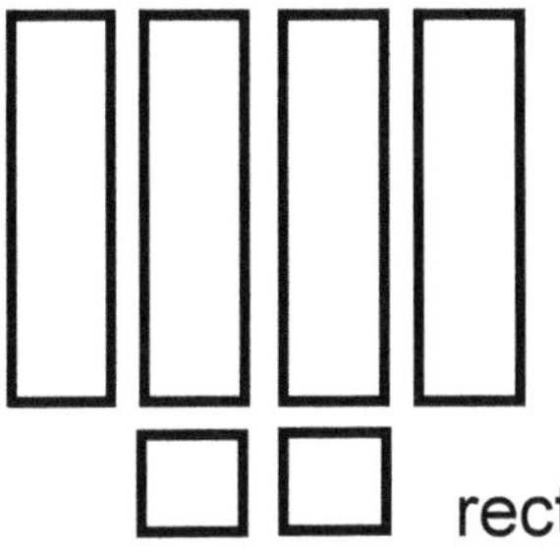

pyramid rectangular prism

4.

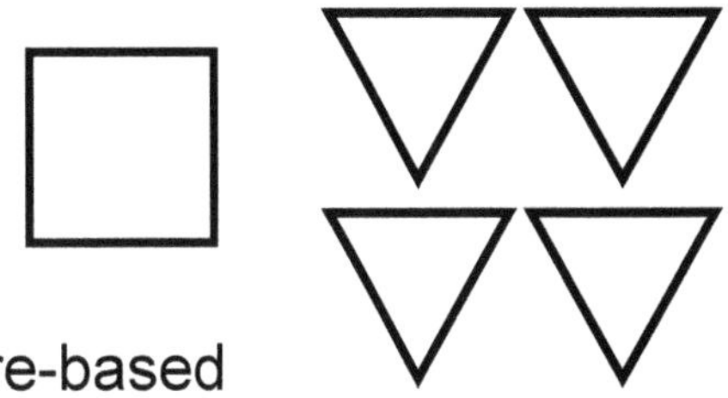

square-based pyramid cube

5.

triangular pyramid rectangular prism

6.

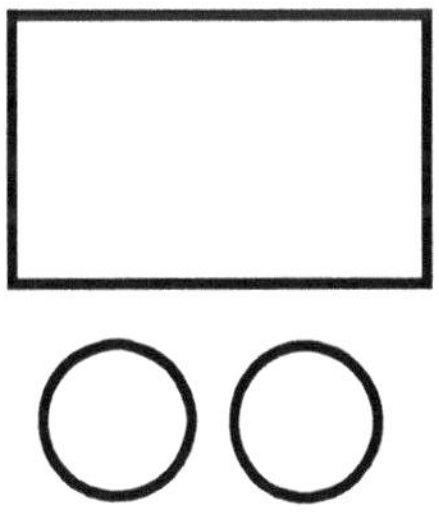

pyramid cylinder

7.

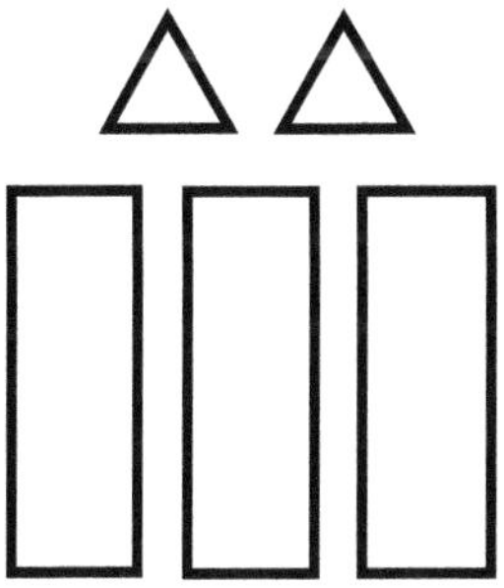

pyramid triangle-based prism

8.

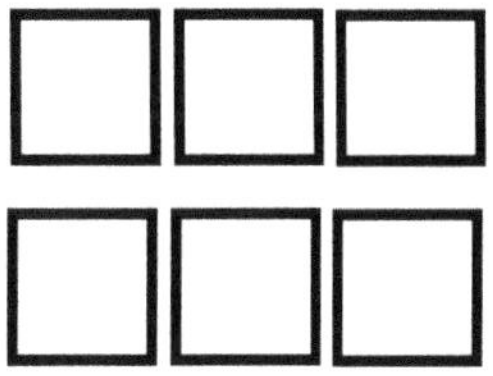

cylinder cube

Exploring Symmetry

A line of symmetry divides a figure into 2 parts that are the exact same size and shape. Some figures have more than 1 line of symmetry. Some figures have no lines of symmetry.

V
F

1 line of symmetry   0 lines of symmetry

1. Examine each letter. Put a circle around the letters that have a line of symmetry. Put an X on the letters that do **not** have a line of symmetry.

B	M	C
E	O	Q
K	U	X

Symmetry Fun

Draw the other half of the spaceship.

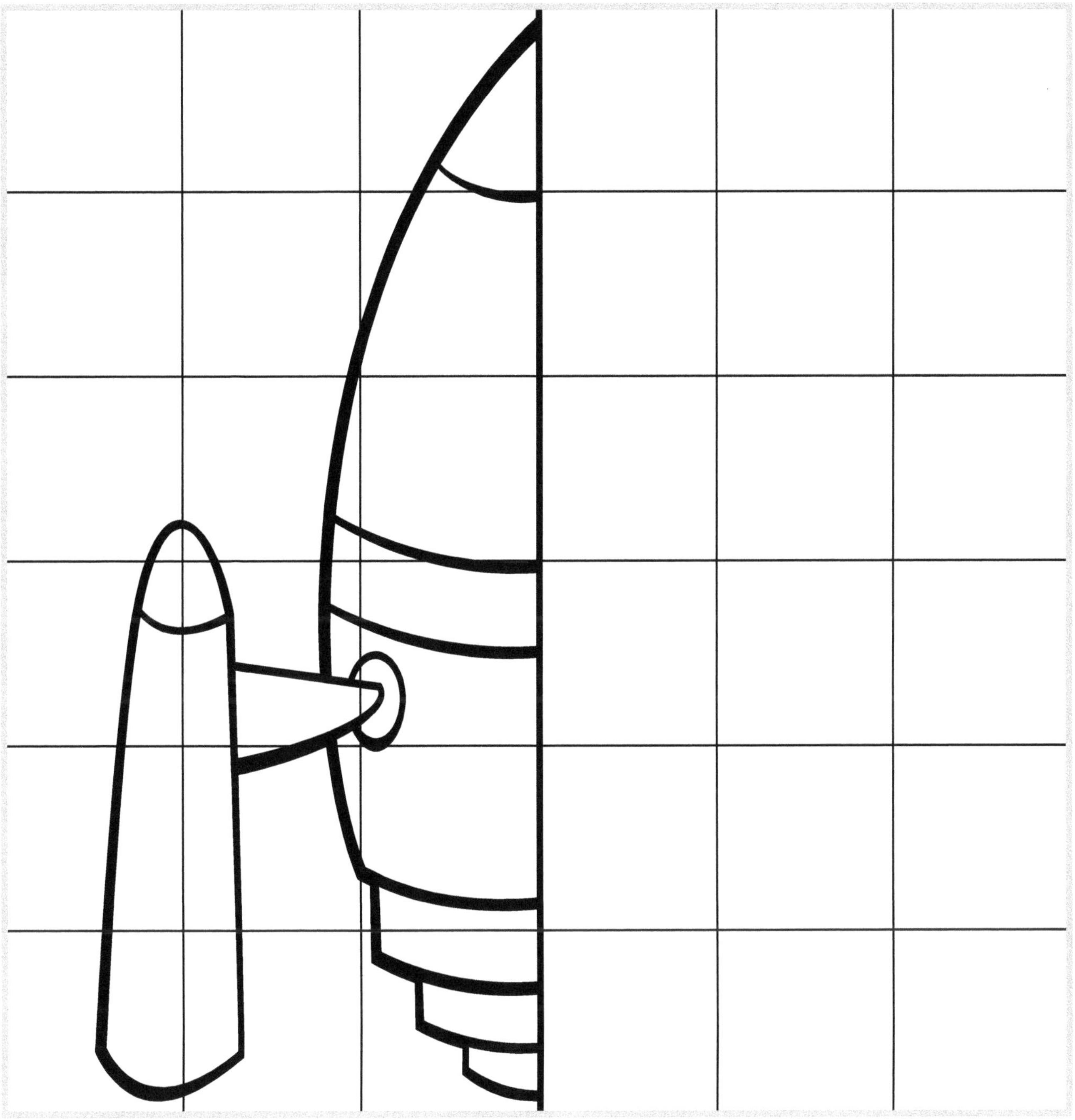

Congruent Figures

Congruent figures have the same shape and size.

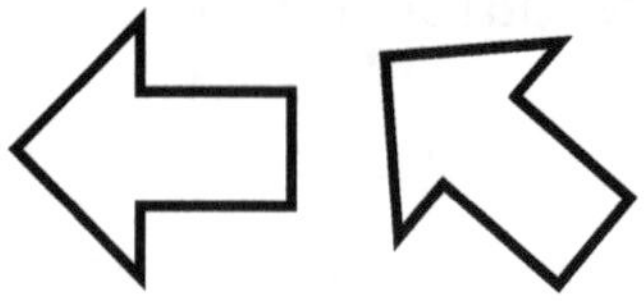

Draw a line connecting the congruent shapes.

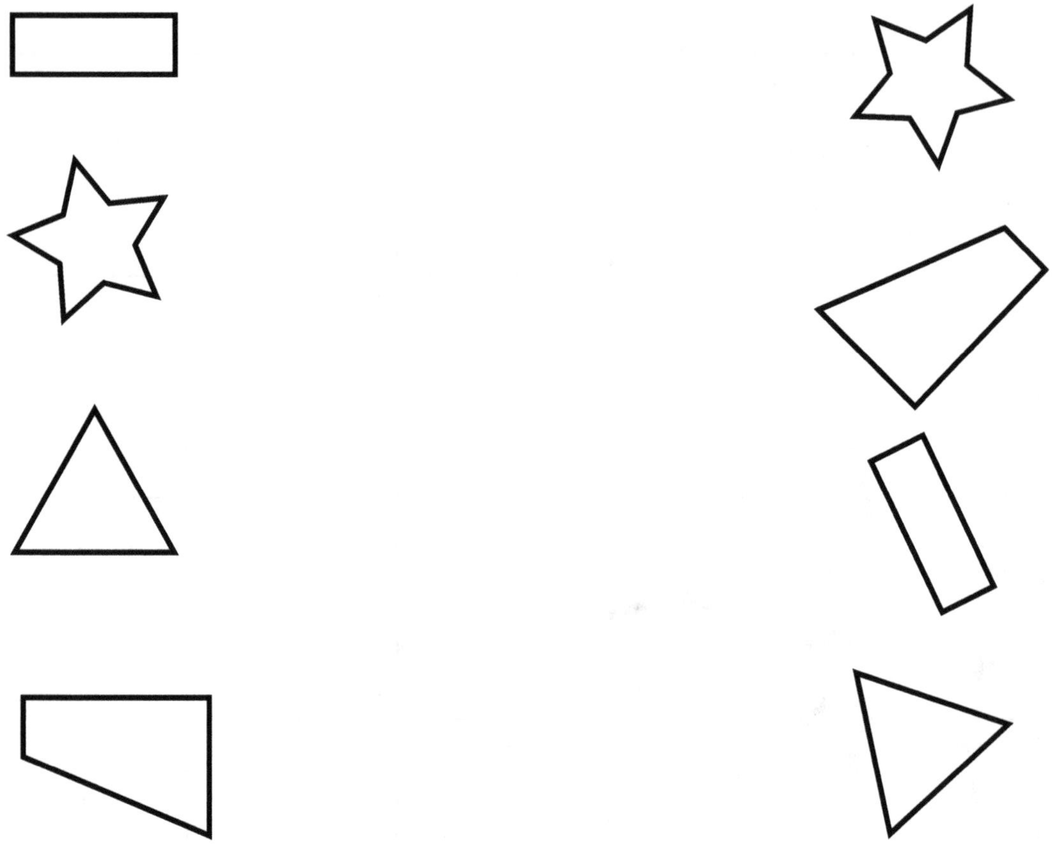

BRAIN STRETCH

How many lines of symmetry? Write the number for each letter.

T___ N___ H___ S___ P___

Flips, Slides, and Turns

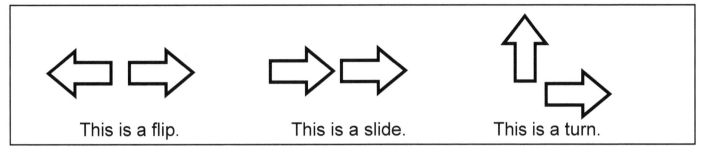

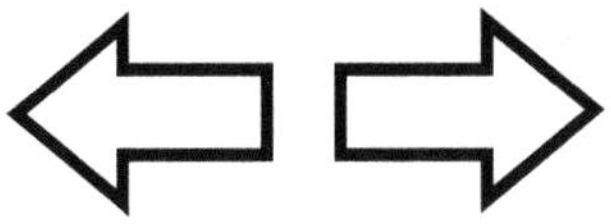

This is a flip.

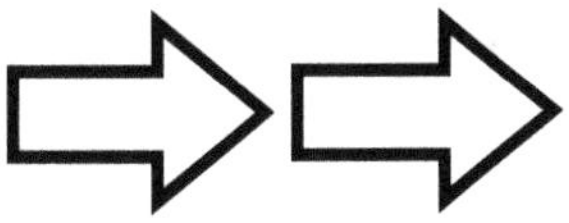

This is a slide.

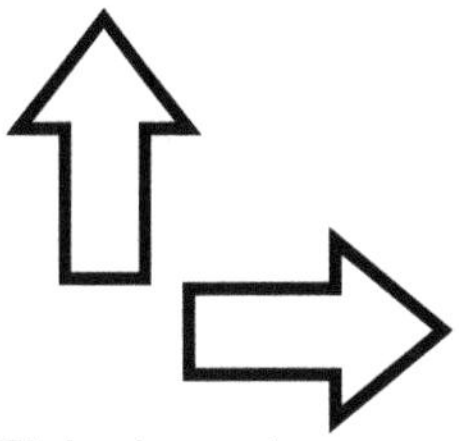

This is a turn.

Write flip, slide, or turn.

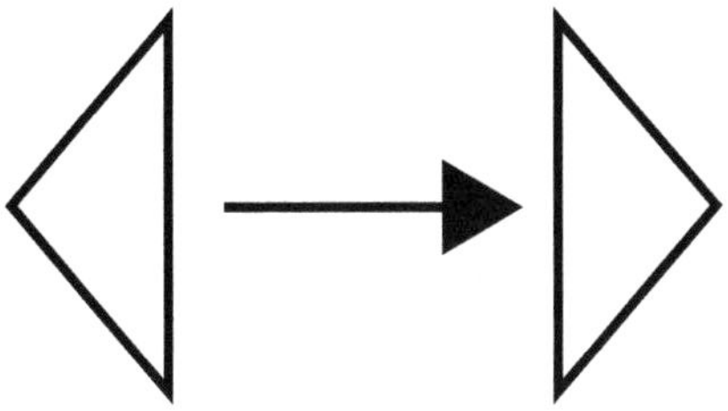

1. ____________________

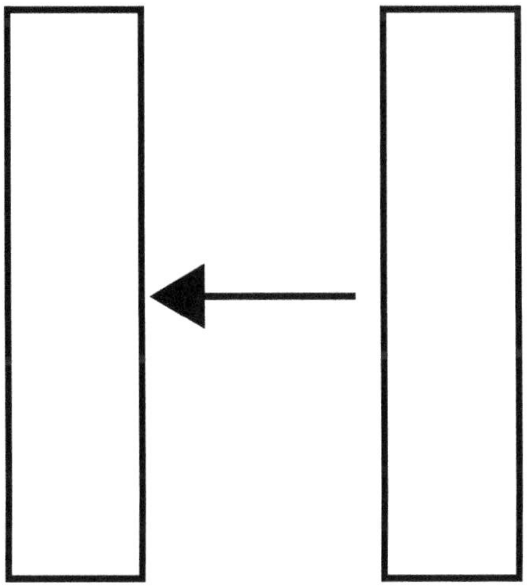

2. ____________________

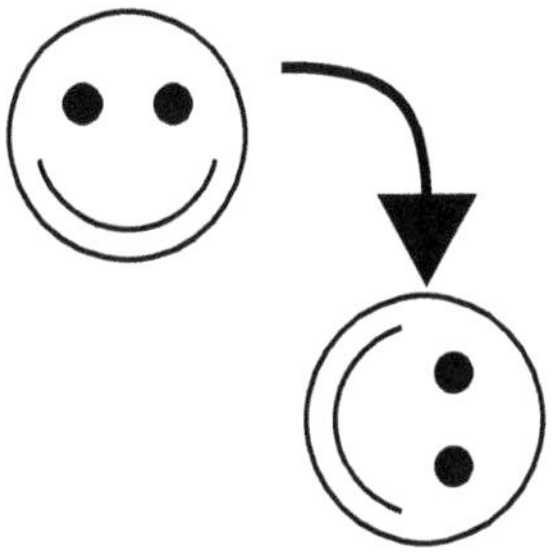

3. ____________________

4. ____________________

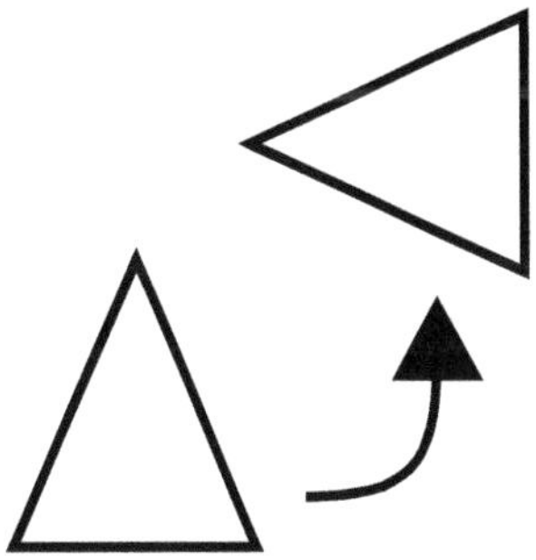

5. ____________________

Exploring Pictographs

A pictograph uses pictures to show data.
A key explains the meaning of the picture.

Key  = 2 votes

Mr. Cooper's class made a pictograph about favourite ways to eat strawberries. Answer the questions.

Favourite Ways to Eat Strawberries

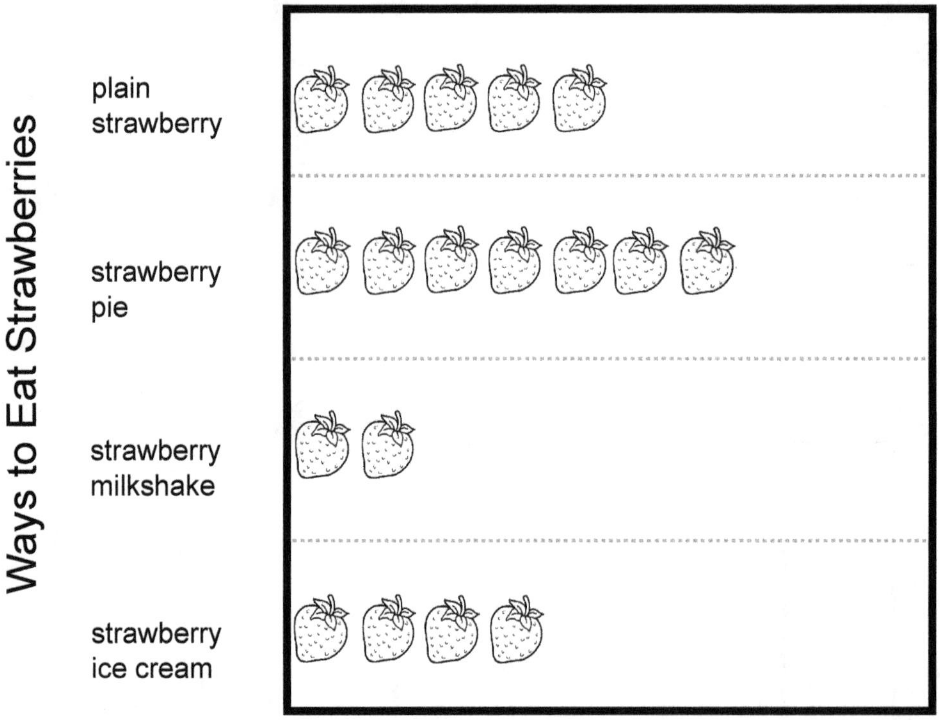
Ways to Eat Strawberries
plain strawberry
strawberry pie
strawberry milkshake
strawberry ice cream

 = 2 votes

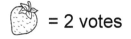

1. What was the most popular way to eat strawberries? ____________________
2. How many votes were made for strawberry pie? ________________
3. How many votes were made in total? ________________

Exploring Bar Graphs

A bar graph shows data using bars.
The bars can go up or across the graph.
Bar graphs are used to compare information.

Use the information from the graph to answer the questions.

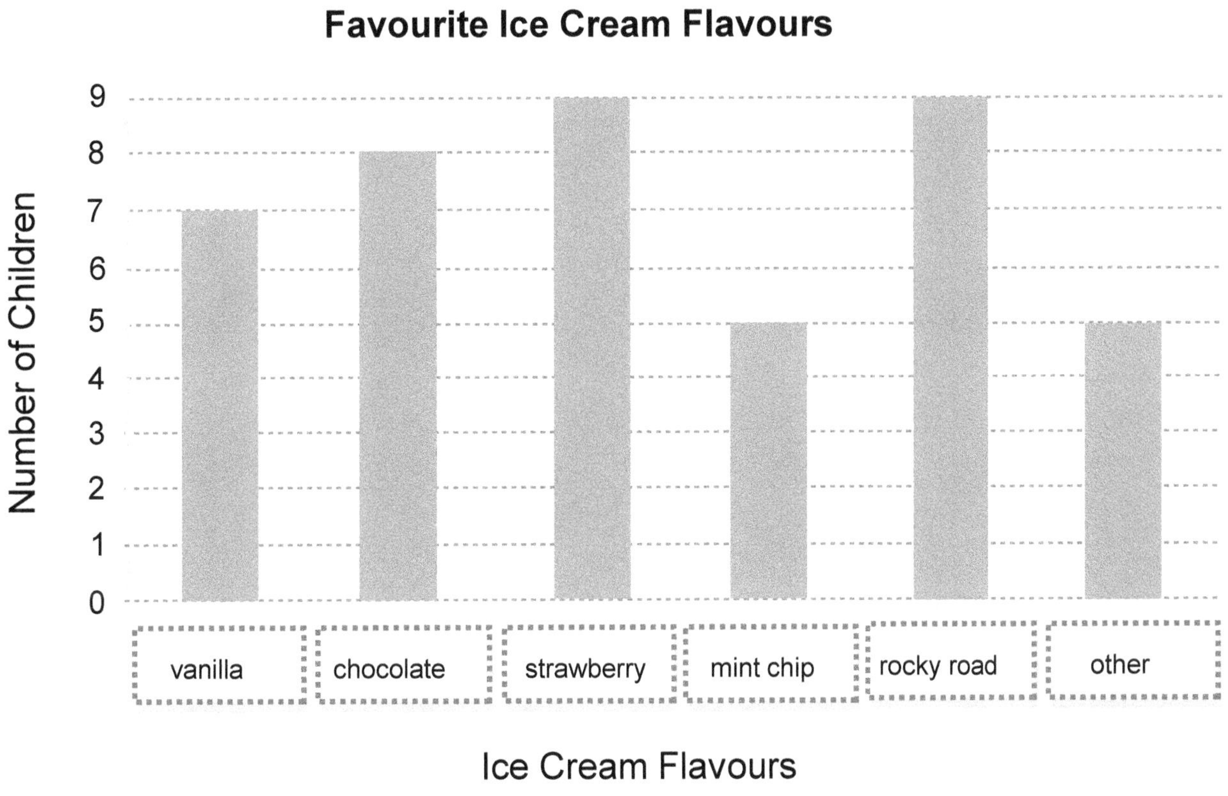

Favourite Ice Cream Flavours
Number of Children
0
1
2
3
4
5
6
7
8
9
vanilla
chocolate
strawberry
mint chip
rocky road
other
Ice Cream Flavours

1. How many children voted altogether? ___________

2. Which flavour was the most popular? ______________________________

3. Which flavour was the least popular? ______________________________

4. What two flavours got the same number of votes? ____________________

5. How many more children preferred strawberry than chocolate? __________

Exploring Bar Graphs

A bar graph shows information or data using bars.
The bars can go up or across the graph.

The two grade 3 classes made a bar graph about favourite activities at recess. Answer the questions.

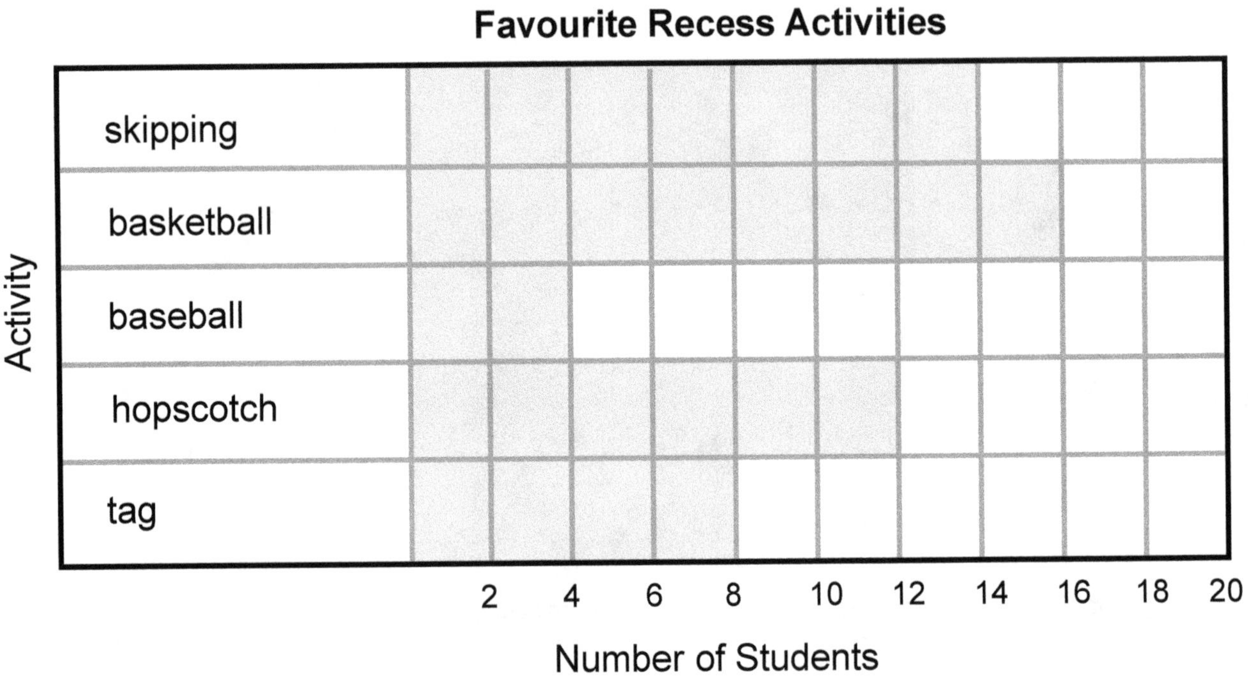
Favourite Recess Activities
Activity
skipping
basketball
baseball
hopscotch
tag
2
4
6
8
10
12
14
16
18
20
Number of Students

1. The most popular recess activity is ______________________.

2. The least popular recess activity is ______________________.

3. How many students liked hopscotch? _______

4. How many more students liked tag than baseball? _______

Exploring Bar Graphs

Ms. Gibson's grade 3 class did a survey about students' favourite pizza toppings.

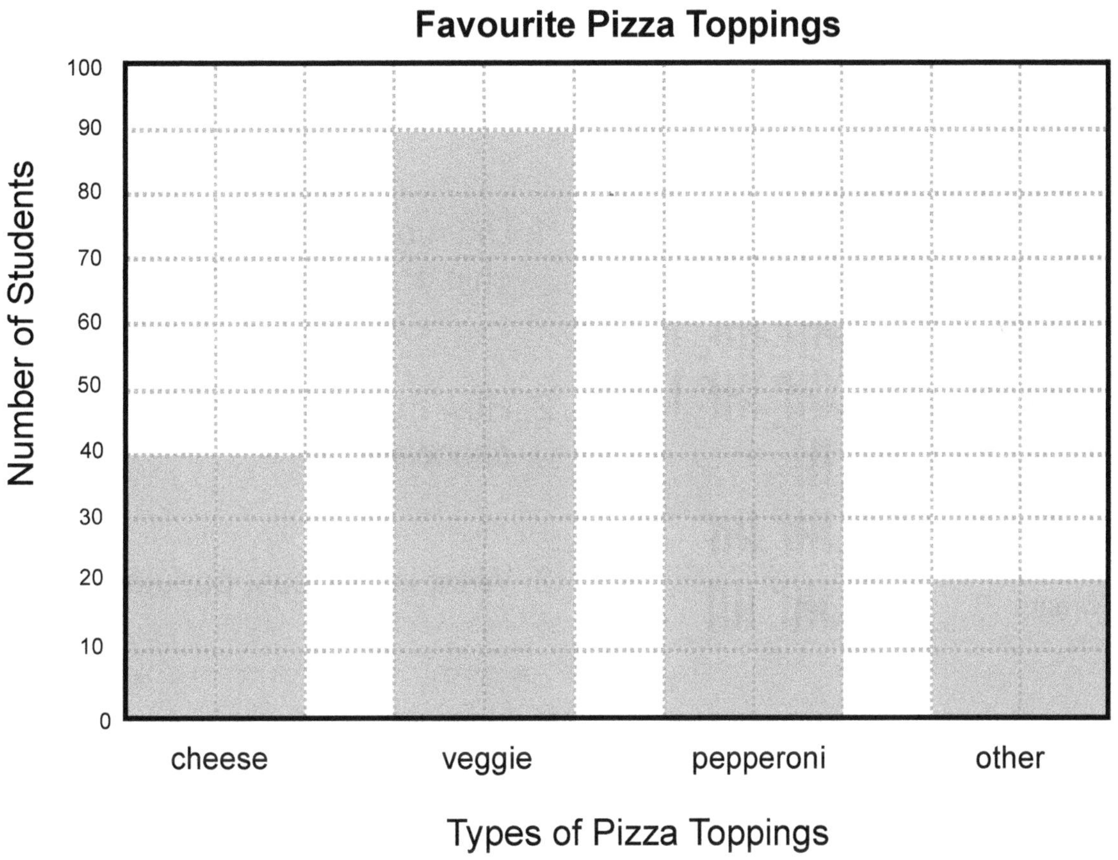

Favourite Pizza Toppings
Number of Students
100
90
80
70
60
50
40
30
20
10
0
cheese
veggie
pepperoni
other
Types of Pizza Toppings

1. Which was most the popular pizza topping? ____________________

2. Cheese was less popular than ____________________.

3. The least popular pizza topping was ____________________.

4. __________ students voted for either cheese or pepperoni.

5. What is your favourite pizza topping? ____________________

Reading Tally Charts

A tally chart counts data in groups of 5.
Each tally or line represents 1.
A group of 5 looks like this.

𝍸 = 5

Answer the questions.

Favourite Cookies

Cookie	Number
Chocolate Chip	𝍸 𝍸 II
Double Chocolate	𝍸 𝍸 I
Animal Crackers	III
Oatmeal Raisin	𝍸 𝍸
Vanilla Cream	𝍸 IIII

1. Did more people choose chocolate chip or animal crackers?

____

2. How many people chose double chocolate?

____

3. What is the least popular cookie?

____

4. How many people voted?

____

Favourite Activities

Activity	Number
Playing Outside	𝍸 𝍸 II
Video Games	𝍸 𝍸 𝍸
Reading	𝍸 III
Watching TV	𝍸 𝍸
Computer	𝍸 II
Listening to Music	𝍸 𝍸 IIII

5. How many people chose playing on the computer?

____

6. How many people chose video games?

____

7. How many people chose reading or watching TV?

____

Favourite Snacks Graph

Tara interviewed two grade 3 classes about their favorite snack. Use the data from the tally chart to complete a bar graph. Answer the questions.

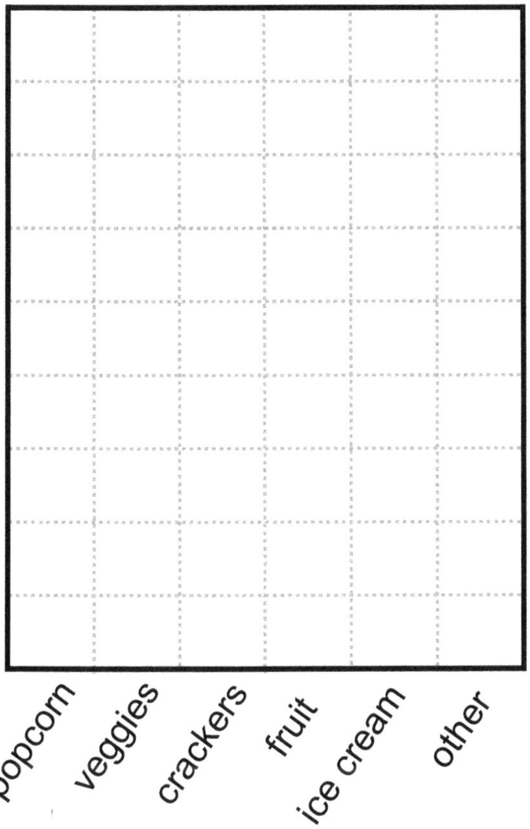
popcorn
veggies
crackers
fruit
ice cream
other

Tally Chart

Snack	Number of Votes
Popcorn	𝍸 𝍸
Veggies	|||
Crackers	𝍸 𝍸 ||
Fruit	𝍸 |||
Ice Cream	𝍸
Other	𝍸 ||||

Make sure the bar graph includes
- a title
- a scale
- a label for the scale

1. What was the most popular snack? ______________________________

2. What was the least popular snack? ______________________________

3. How many more students voted for crackers instead of fruit? __________

4. If 6 more students voted for ice cream, how many votes would there be for ice cream? __________

5. How many students voted in the survey? __________

Favourite Recess Activities Graph

Michael surveyed the children in two grade 3 classes about their favourite recess activity

1. Skipping got 14 votes, baseball got 16 votes, and basketball got 12 votes. Create a tally chart to show the information from the survey.

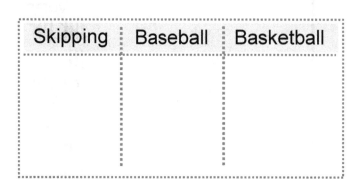

Skipping	Baseball	Basketball

2. Complete the horizontal bar graph to show the information from Michael. Make sure you label.

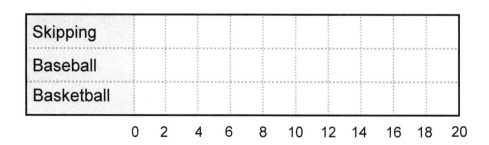

Skipping										
Baseball										
Basketball										

0 2 4 6 8 10 12 14 16 18 20

3. What was the most popular activity? ____________________

4. What was the least popular activity? ____________________

5. How many people voted in the survey? ____________

6. Grade 3 students voted for ______________ more than ______________.

Favourite Vegetables Bar Graph

Mr. Clark's class took a survey of favourite vegetables.
Use the data from the tally chart to complete the bar graph.

Favourite Vegetables

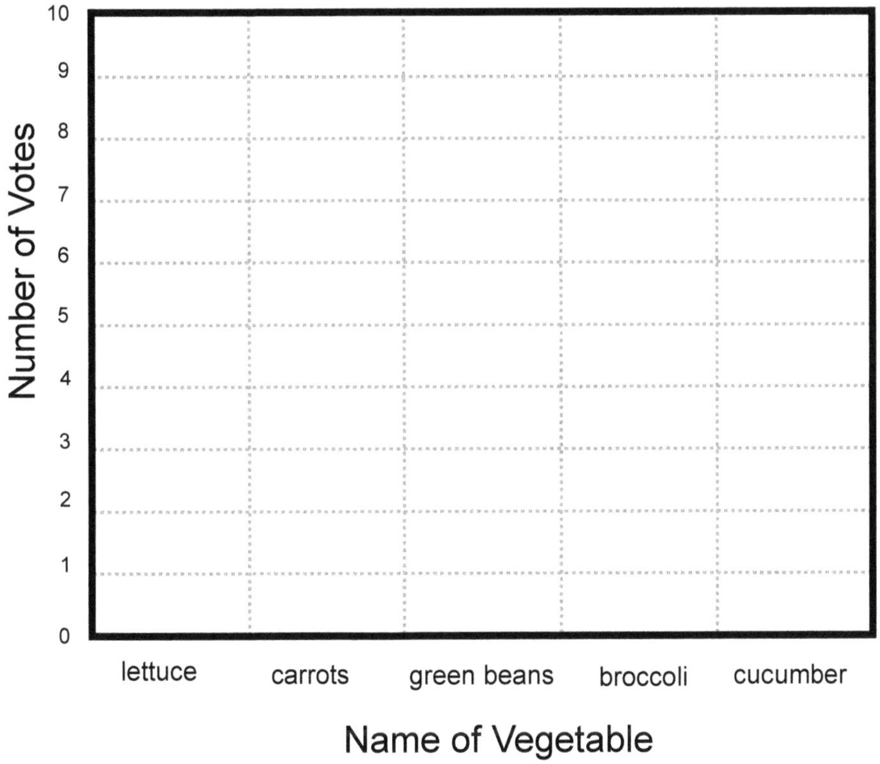

Number of Votes
10
9
8
7
6
5
4
3
2
1
0
lettuce
carrots
green beans
broccoli
cucumber
Name of Vegetable

Tally Chart

Vegetable	Number of Votes
Lettuce	2
Carrots	7
Green Beans	8
Broccoli	10
Cucumber	5

1. What is the most popular vegetable? ____________________

2. How many fewer people chose carrots than broccoli? __________

3. List the vegetables in order from the vegetable with the fewest votes to the vegetable with the most votes. ______________________________

____

4. How many people chose either lettuce or green beans? __________

5. How many students took part in this survey altogether? __________

6. How many students did not vote for cucumber? __________

Exploring Ordered Pairs

An ordered pair describes a point on a grid. It has 2 numbers in a certain order.

- The first number tells how many units to count to the right.
- The second number tells how many units to count up.

Hint: Always start counting at the bottom left corner, at 0.

Count 1 unit right. Go up 3 units. The ordered pair is (1, 3). 

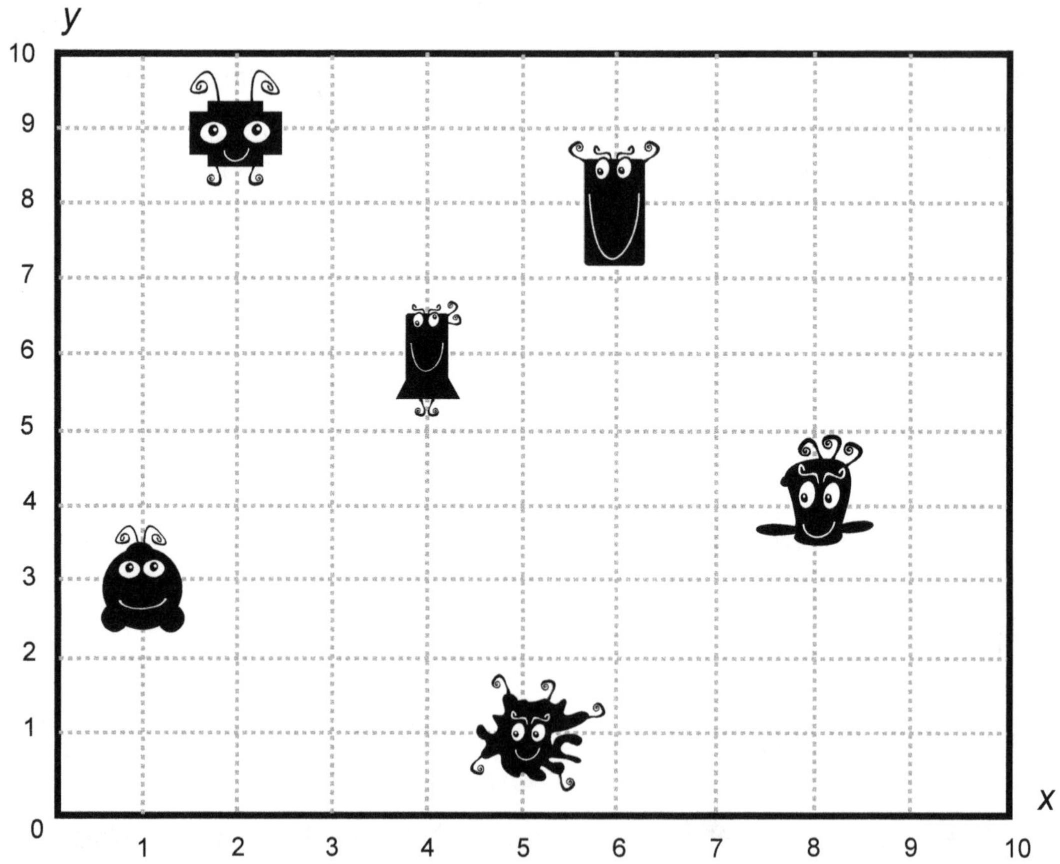

y
10
9
8
7
6
5
4
3
2
1
0
1
2
3
4
5
6
7
8
9
10
x

1. Look at the grid. Write the ordered pair for each creature.

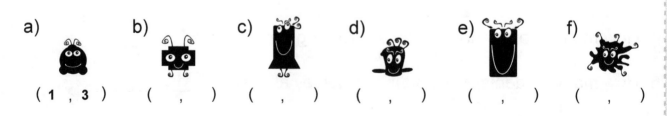

a)  (1 , 3)

b)  (,)

c)  (,)

d)  (,)

e)  (,)

f)  (,)

Exploring Ordered Pairs (continued)

2. Draw the shapes on the grid at the locations given by the ordered pairs.

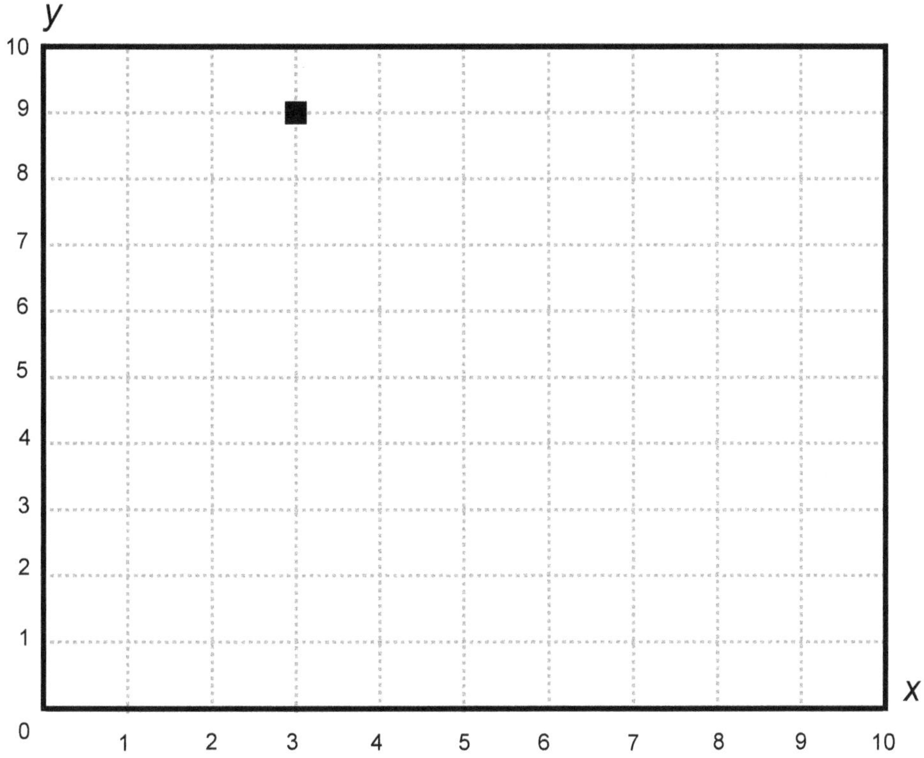
y
10
9
8
7
6
5
4
3
2
1
0
1 2 3 4 5 6 7 8 9 10
x

Ordered Pairs

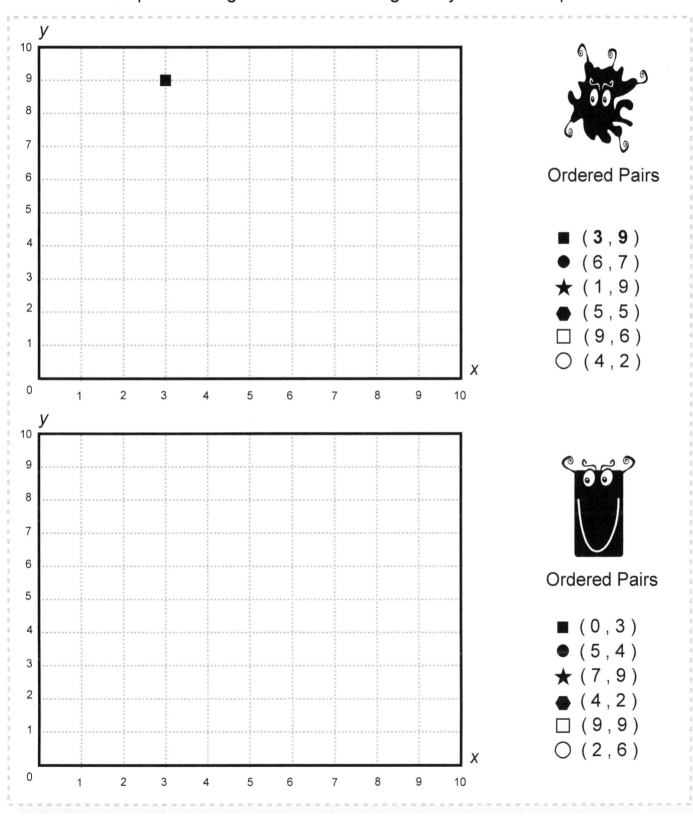

- ■ (**3** , **9**)
- ● (6 , 7)
- ★ (1 , 9)
- ⬢ (5 , 5)
- □ (9 , 6)
- ○ (4 , 2)

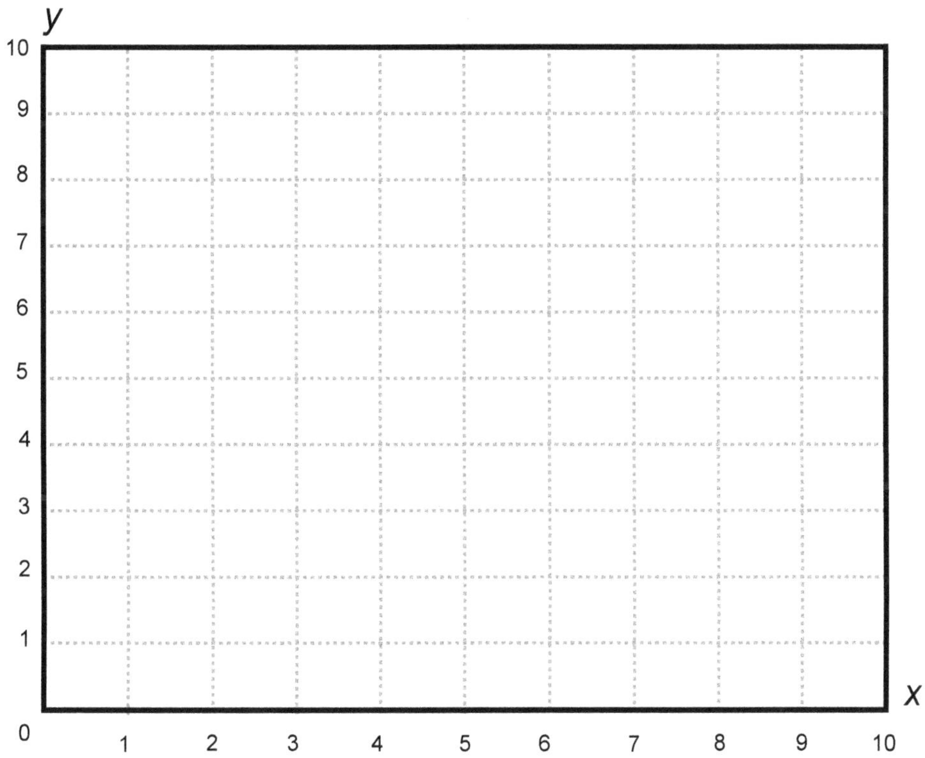
y
10
9
8
7
6
5
4
3
2
1
0
1 2 3 4 5 6 7 8 9 10
x

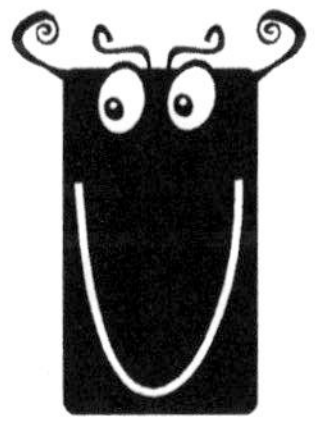

Ordered Pairs

- ■ (0 , 3)
- ● (5 , 4)
- ★ (7 , 9)
- ⬢ (4 , 2)
- □ (9 , 9)
- ○ (2 , 6)

Exploring Measurement

1. What would be the best unit of measure for the following?

kilometre	metre	centimetre

The length of a classroom.	
The width of a stamp.	
The distance between two cities.	
The length of a book.	
The length of your arm.	
The length of a bus.	

2. Draw a line from the item being measured to the best measurement tool for the job.

The amount of sugar in a cake recipe	ruler
The weight of 3 bunches of bananas	thermometer
The temperature on a hot day	measuring cup
The length of a caterpillar	scale

Exploring Perimeter

To find the distance around (perimeter) add the sides.

5 m + 5 m + 3 m + 3 m = 16 m

The distance around is 16 metres.

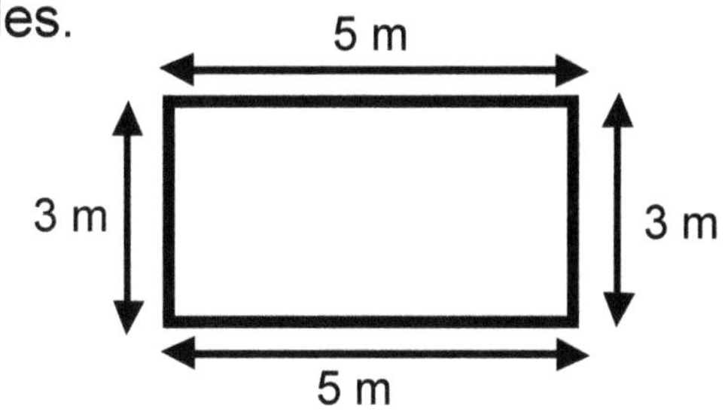
5 m
3 m
3 m
5 m

What is the perimeter of each shape? Use **m** for metres.

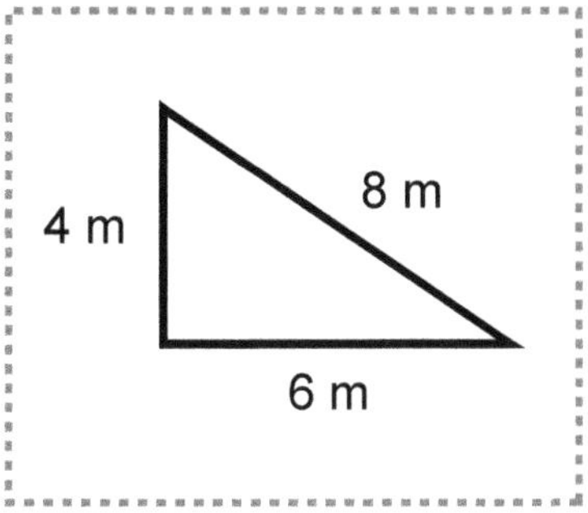
4 m
8 m
6 m

___ + ___ + ___ = ___ m

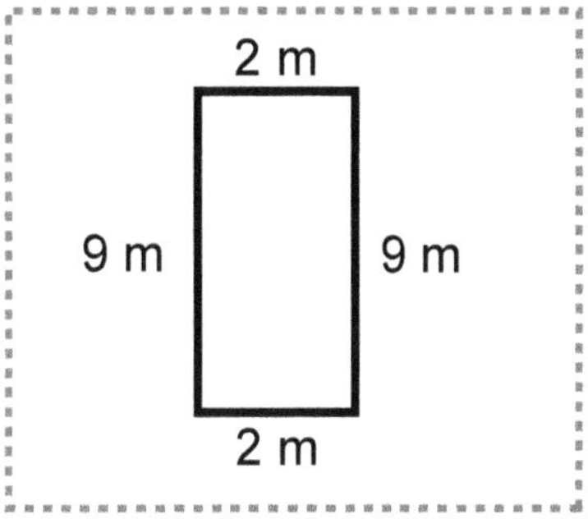
2 m
9 m
9 m
2 m

___ + ___ + ___ + ___ = ___ m

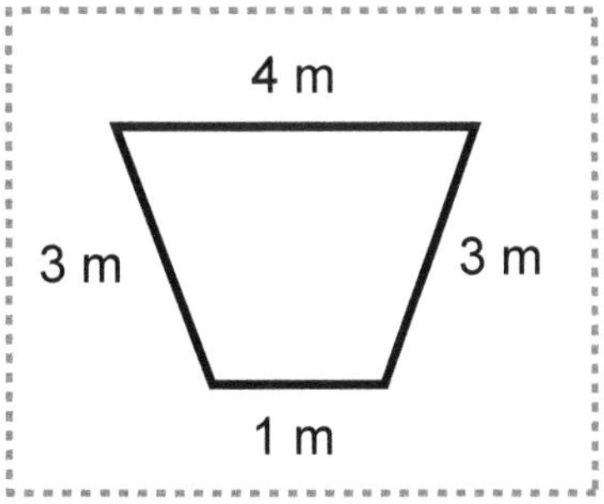
4 m
3 m
3 m
1 m

___ + ___ + ___ + ___ = ___ m

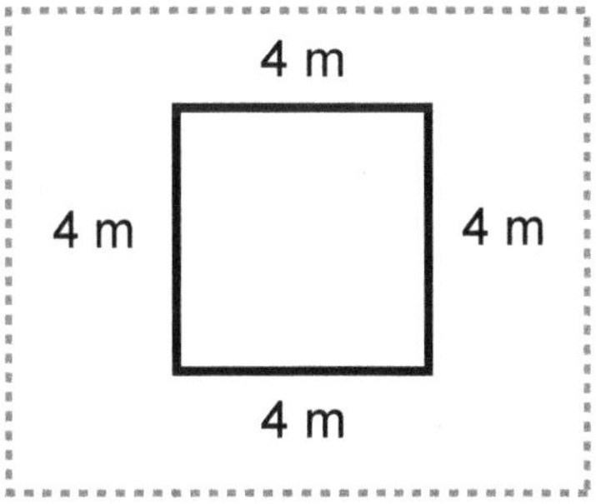
4 m
4 m
4 m
4 m

___ + ___ + ___ + ___ = ___ m

Exploring Perimeter

The perimeter is the distance around a figure. Find the perimeter of each figure by counting the units around each figure.

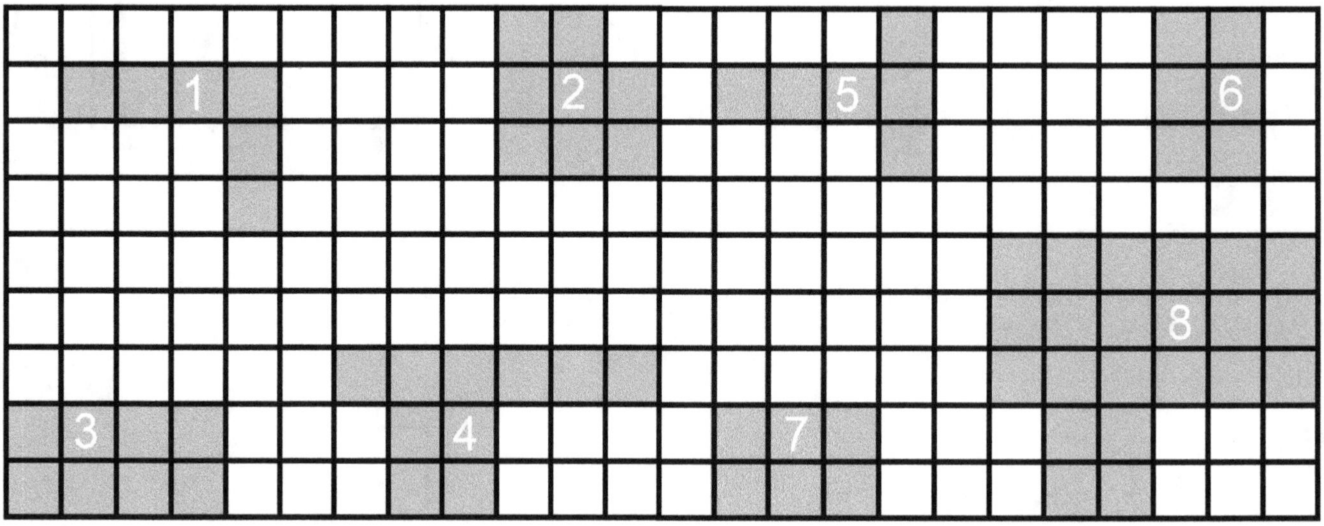
1
2
5
6
8
3
4
7

1. The perimeter of figure 1 is ___ units.
2. The perimeter of figure 2 is ___ units.
3. The perimeter of figure 3 is ___ units.
4. The perimeter of figure 4 is ___ units.
5. The perimeter of figure 5 is ___ units.
6. The perimeter of figure 6 is ___ units.
7. The perimeter of figure 7 is ___ units.
8. The perimeter of figure 8 is ___ units.

BRAIN STRETCH

Both of these figures have 12 squares.
Circle the figure with the shortest perimeter.

a) 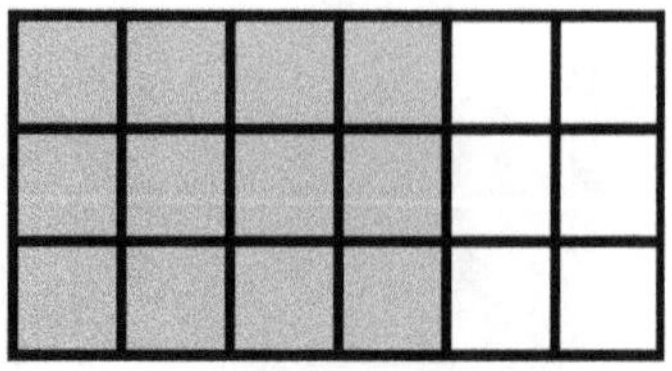

b) 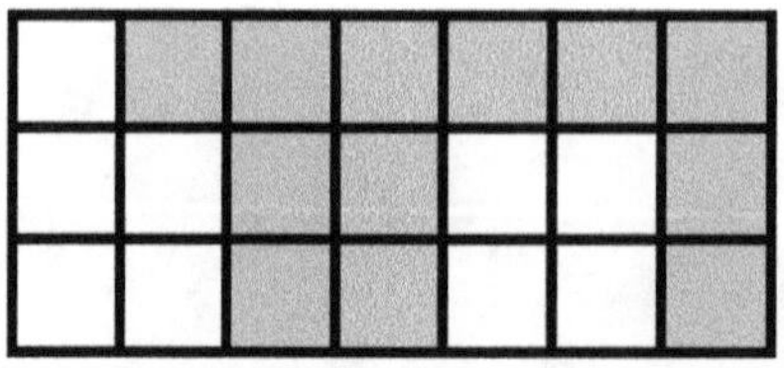

Exploring Area

Area is the number of units that covers a figure.

1 square  = 1 unit.

Count the number of square units that cover the figure.
The area of the shaded shape is 7 square units.

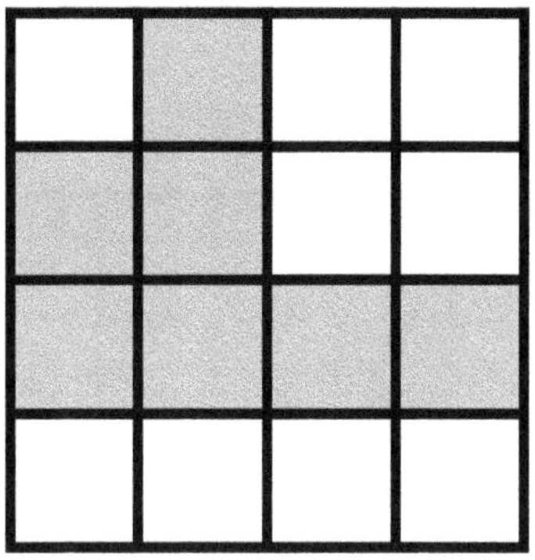

1. Find the area of each shaded figure.

a) 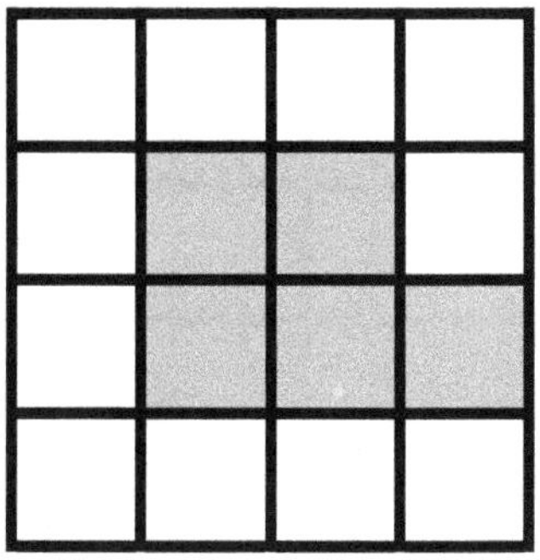

Area = _____ square units

b) 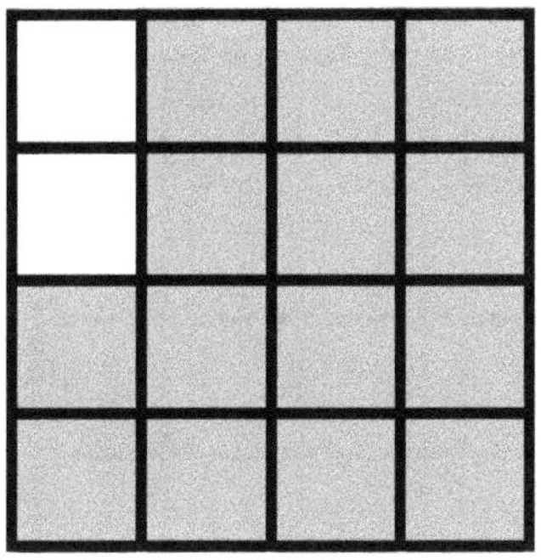

Area = _____ square units

c) 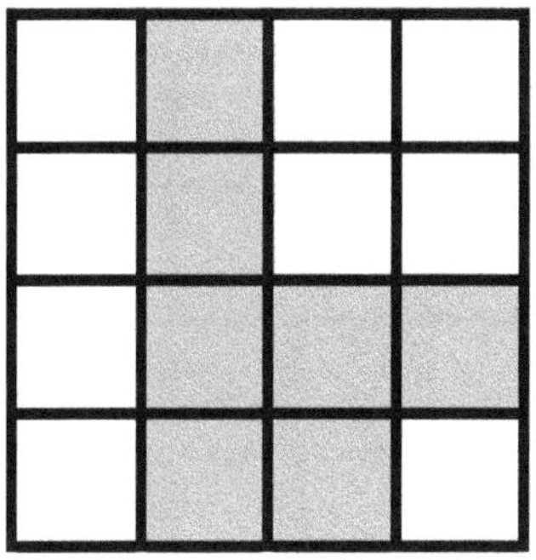

Area = _____ square units

d) 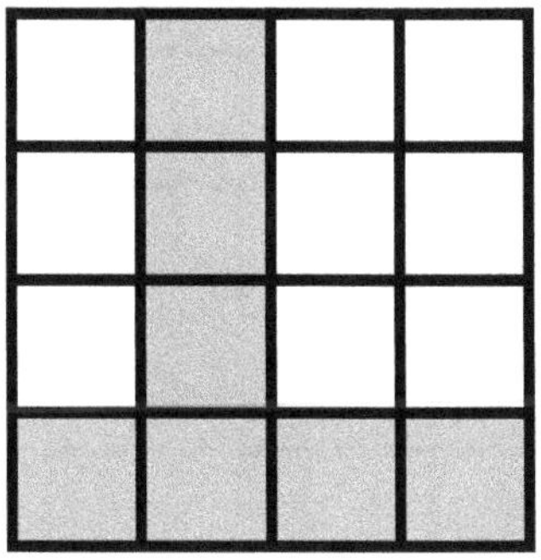

Area = _____ square units

e) 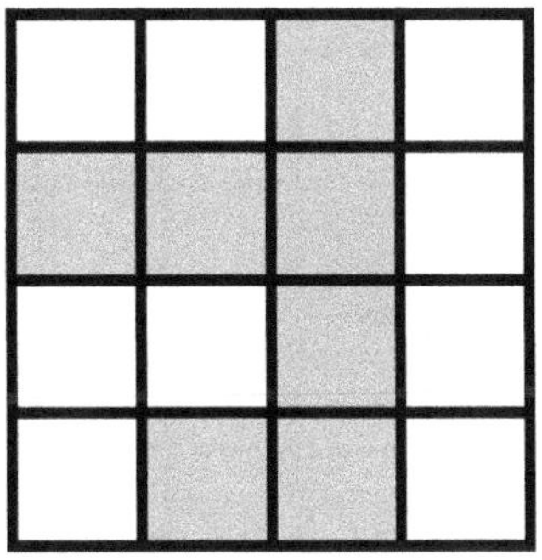

Area = _____ square units

f) 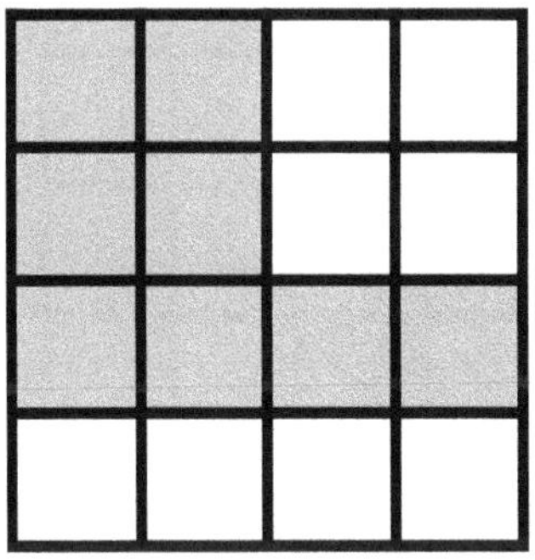

Area = _____ square units

Exploring Area (continued)

2. Find the area of each figure.

a)

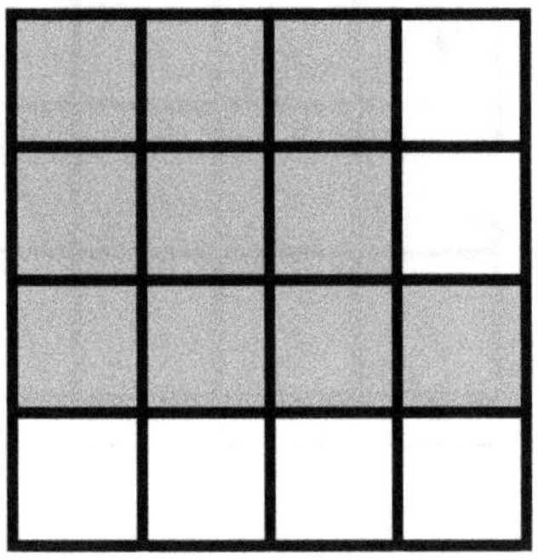

Area = ______ square units

b)

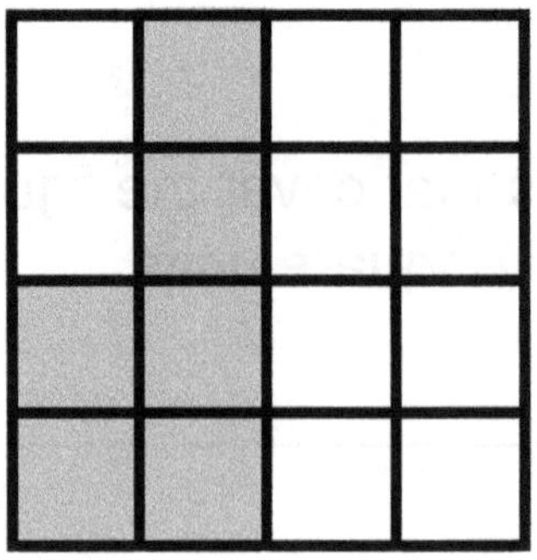

Area = ______ square units

c)

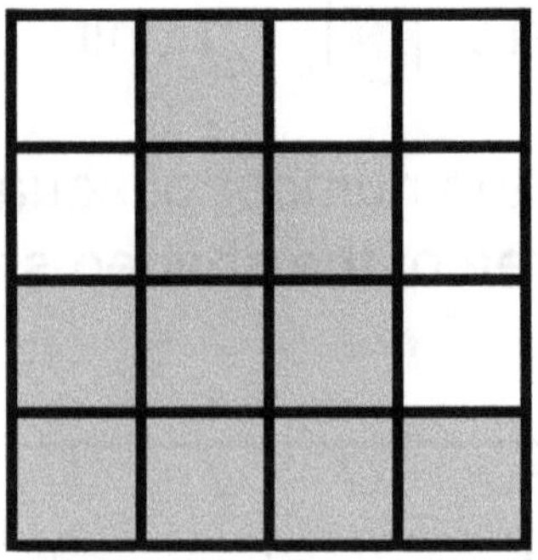

Area = ______ square units

d)

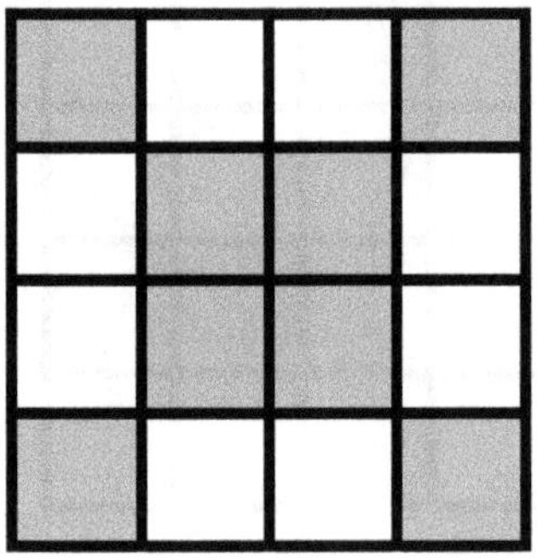

Area = ______ square units

e)

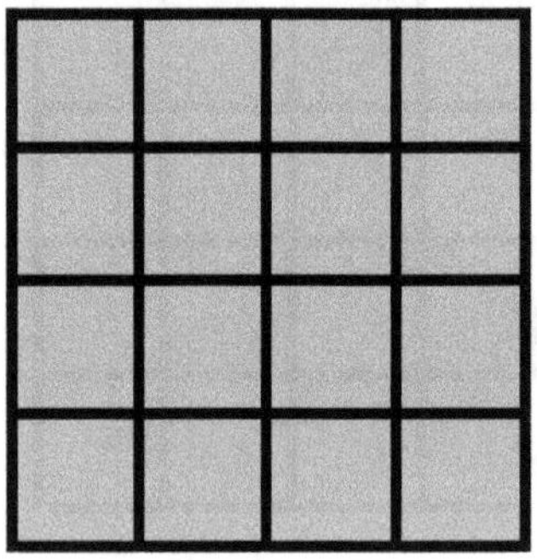

Area = ______ square units

f)

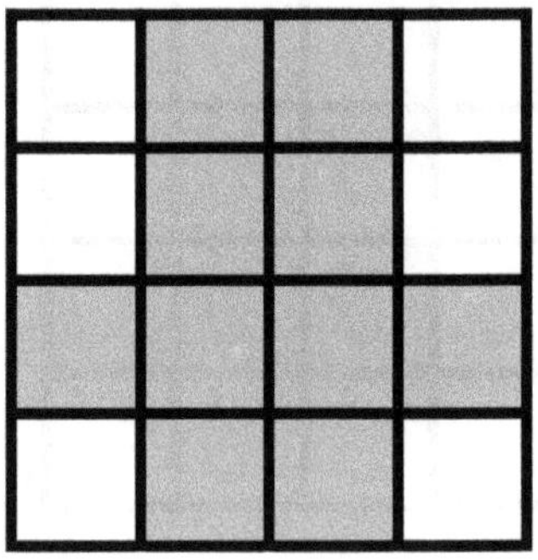

Area = ______ square units

g)

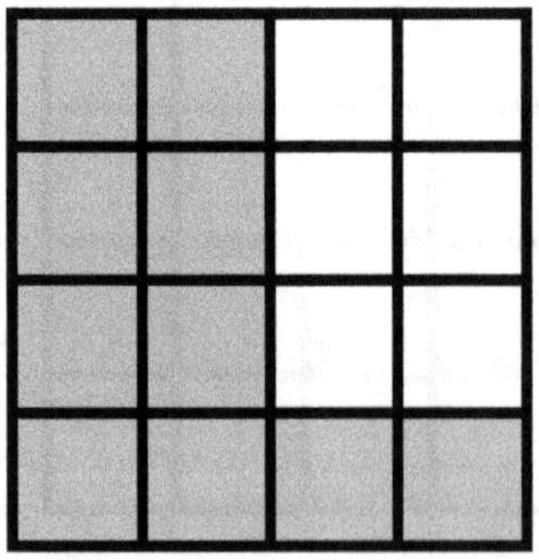

Area = ______ square units

h)

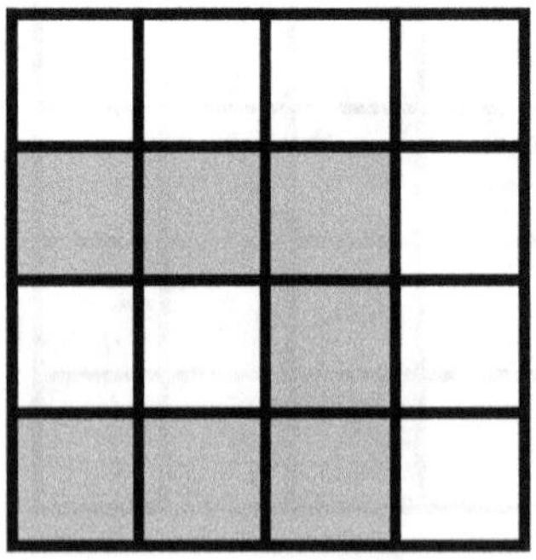

Area = ______ square units

i)

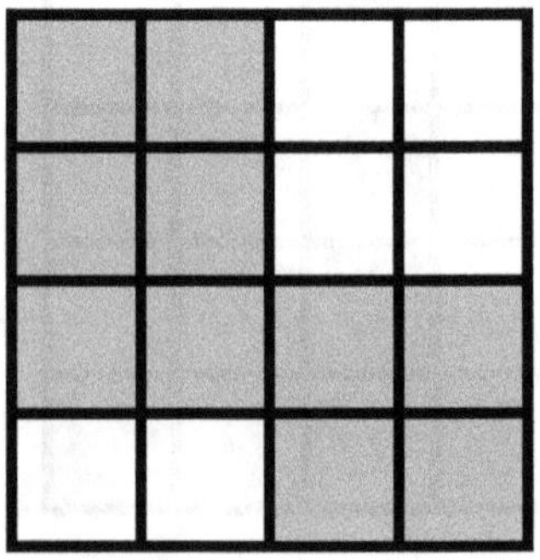

Area = ______ square units

Exploring Length

Write the length in centimetres. Write **cm** for centimetres.

1.

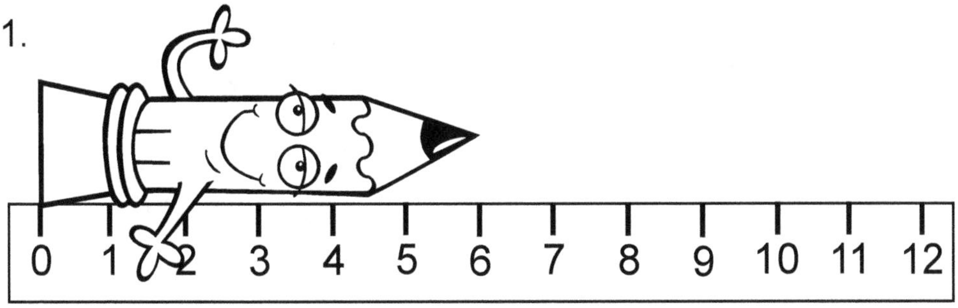
0 1 2 3 4 5 6 7 8 9 10 11 12

cm

2.

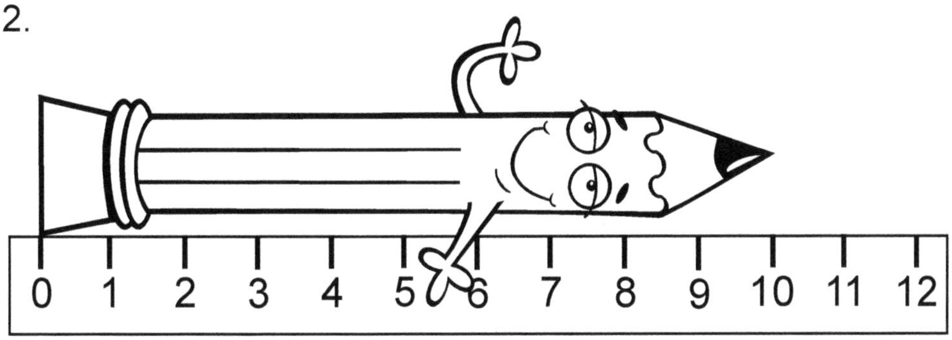
0 1 2 3 4 5 6 7 8 9 10 11 12

3.

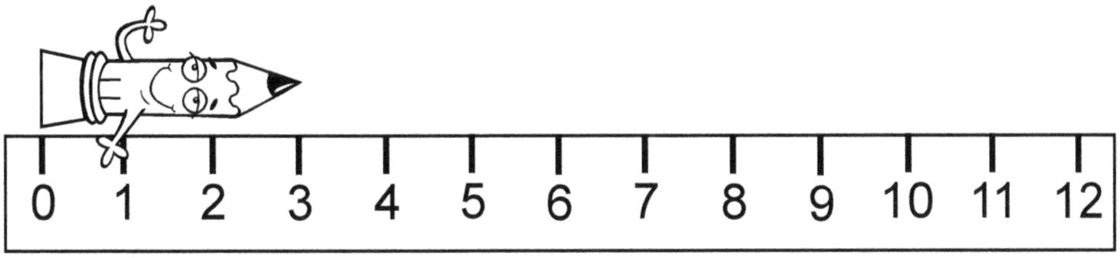
0 1 2 3 4 5 6 7 8 9 10 11 12

4.

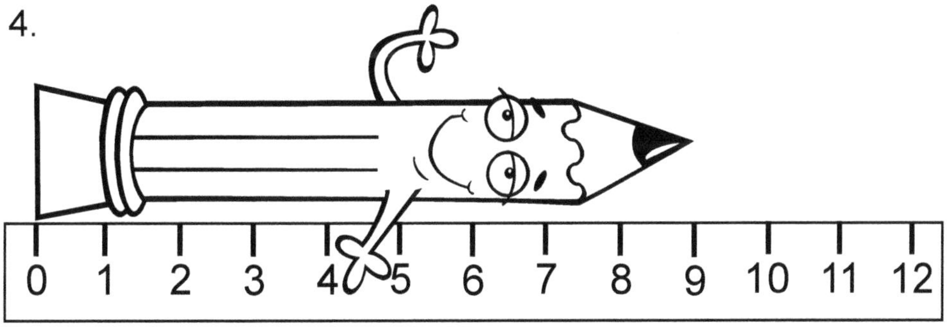
0 1 2 3 4 5 6 7 8 9 10 11 12

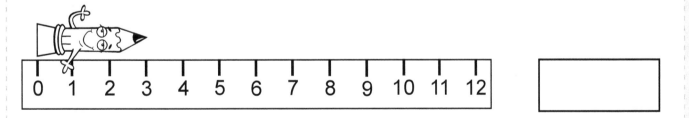

What Time Is It?

A clock shows time using numbers and hands.
The face of a clock shows the numbers 1 to 12.
It takes 5 minutes for the long minute hand to move from one number to the next.

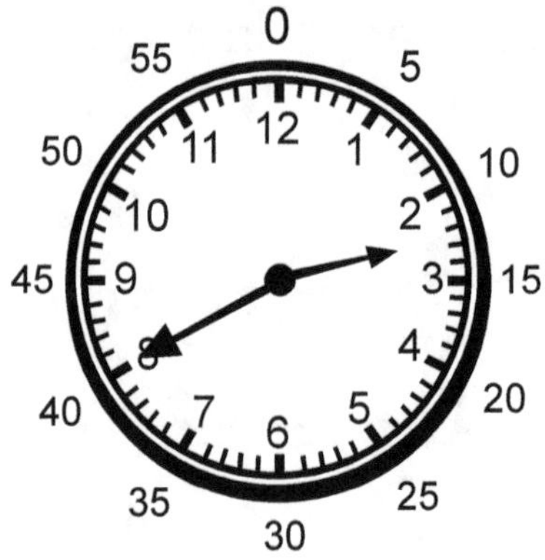
0
5
10
15
20
25
30
35
40
45
50
55
12 1 2 3 4 5 6 7 8 9 10 11

The time is 2:40.

Highlight the hour hand blue.
Highlight the minute hand red.

1.

____ : ____

2.

____ : ____

3.

____ : ____

4.

____ : ____

5.

____ : ____

6.

____ : ____

Drawing the Hands

Draw the two hands on the clock to show the time.
Highlight the hour hand blue. Highlight the minute hand red.

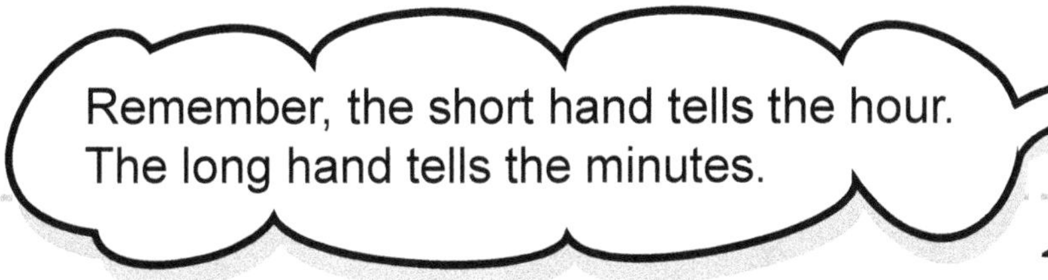

Remember, the short hand tells the hour.
The long hand tells the minutes.

1. 
12 1 2 3 4 5 6 7 8 9 10 11

10 : 25

2. 
12 1 2 3 4 5 6 7 8 9 10 11

ten minutes after six

3. 
12 1 2 3 4 5 6 7 8 9 10 11

20 minutes before 4

4. 
12 1 2 3 4 5 6 7 8 9 10 11

half past 7

5. 
12 1 2 3 4 5 6 7 8 9 10 11

25 minutes after 2

6. 
12 1 2 3 4 5 6 7 8 9 10 11

6 : 30

7. 
12 1 2 3 4 5 6 7 8 9 10 11

five minutes after eight

8. 
12 1 2 3 4 5 6 7 8 9 10 11

2 : 40

Elapsed Time

Elapsed time is the amount of time that has passed from the start of a time period to the end of a time period.

Start Time

End Time

25 minutes have elapsed.

Write the start time and the end time.

1\.

Start Time

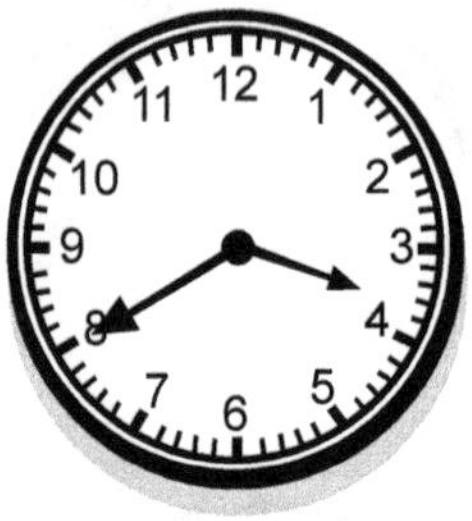

_____ : _____ pm

End Time

_____ : _____ pm

What is the elapsed time?

☐

minutes have passed

2\.

Start Time

_____ : _____ pm

End Time

_____ : _____ pm

What is the elapsed time?

☐

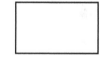

hour has passed

3\.

Start Time

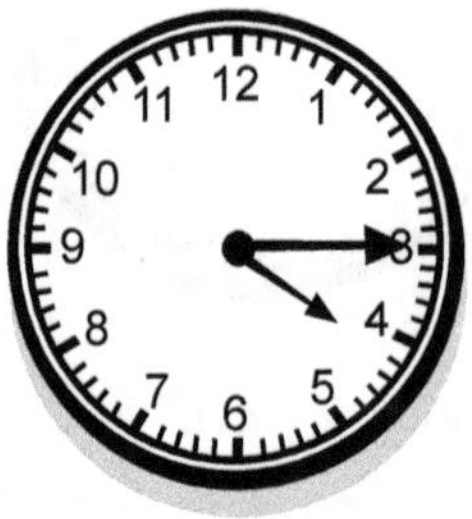

_____ : _____ pm

End Time

_____ : _____ pm

What is the elapsed time?

☐

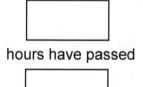

hours have passed

☐

minutes have passed

Basketball Fun

1. Charlie practices basketball for 25 minutes every night.Complete the chart to show his start and end time for each practice.

a.m. refers to before midday
p.m. refers to after midday

Day of the week	Start Time	Finish Time
Sunday	5:45 p.m.	
Monday		6:20 p.m.
Tuesday	5:35 p.m.	
Wednesday		7:25 p.m.
Thursday	5:40 p.m.	
Friday		4:55 p.m.
Saturday	5:05 p.m.	

2. How many minutes did Charlie practice shooting basketballs for the whole week? ____________________

BRAIN STRETCH

Fill in the correct time. Be sure to include a.m. or p.m.

a) This afternoon, Megan started her homework at:

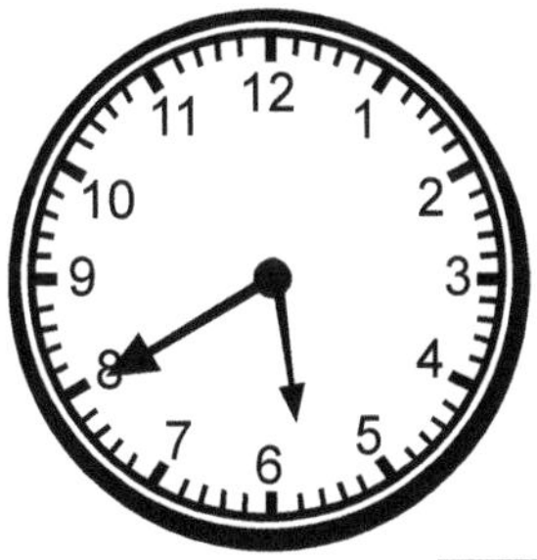
12
1
2
3
4
5
6
7
8
9
10
11

_____ : _____ ☐

b) Megan did her homework after school for 1 hour and 10 minutes. What time did she finish her homework?

12
1
2
3
4
5
6
7
8
9
10
11

_____ : _____ ☐

Using a Schedule

Mr K.'s class took a trip to the aquarium. Use the schedule of aquarium activities to answer the questions.

Aquarium Activity Schedule

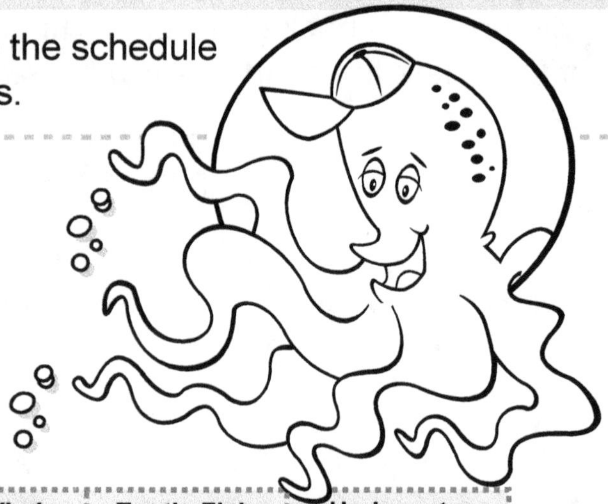

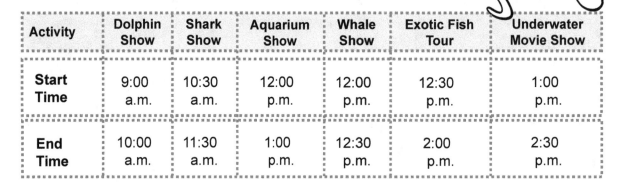

Activity	Dolphin Show	Shark Show	Aquarium Show	Whale Show	Exotic Fish Tour	Underwater Movie Show
Start Time	9:00 a.m.	10:30 a.m.	12:00 p.m.	12:00 p.m.	12:30 p.m.	1:00 p.m.
End Time	10:00 a.m.	11:30 a.m.	1:00 p.m.	12:30 p.m.	2:00 p.m.	2:30 p.m.

1. Which activities start between 9:00 a.m. and 11:30 a.m.?

____

2. Which aquarium activities have an elapsed time of 1 and a half hours?

____

3. Which activities start at 12:00 p.m.?

____

4. Create a schedule for an aquarium visit.

Activity	Start Time	End Time

Reading a Calendar

Use the calendar to answer the questions.

March

S	M	T	W	T	F	S
		1	2	3	4	5
6	7	8	9	10	11	12
13	14	15	16	17	18	19
20	21	22	23	24	25	26
27	28	29	30	31		

1. What day of the week is March 14?

____

2. How many Wednesdays are there in March?

____

3. What is the date 1 week and 2 days after March 3?

____

4. What is the date of the first Tuesday in March?

____

5. On what day of the week will the next month begin?

____

6. What is the date of the third Monday?

____

June

S	M	T	W	T	F	S
			1	2	3	4
5	6	7	8	9	10	11
12	13	14	15	16	17	18
19	20	21	22	23	24	25
26	27	28	29	30		

7. Katherine will have a birthday party in 4 days. Today is June 6. What is the date of her birthday?

____

8. Alexander's karate tournament is in two weeks. Today is June 11. What date is the karate tournament?

____

9. Jane will go on a trip in 6 days. Today is June 10. On what date will Jane go on her trip?

____

10. Carolyn leaves for New York in 9 days. Today is June 17. What date will she leave?

____

Amazing Work!

____

You are a
math all-star!

Answers

Counting by 3s p. 1
1. 12, 15, 18, 21, 24 **2.** 27, 30, 33, 36, 39, 42 **3.** 66, 69, 72, 75, 78, 81 **4.** 45, 48, 51, 54, 57, 60
5. 87, 90, 93, 96, 99 **6.** 39, 36, 33, 30, 27 **7.** 15, 12, 9, 6, 3, 0 **8.** 66, 63, 60, 57, 54, 51 **9.** 96, 93, 90, 87, 84, 81
10. 36, 33, 30, 27, 24, 21

Counting by 4s p. 2
1. 16, 20, 24, 28, 32 **2.** 56, 60, 64, 68, 72, 76 **3.** 80, 84, 88, 92, 96, 100 **4.** 72, 76, 80, 84, 88, 92
5. 36, 40, 44, 48, 52, 56 **6.** 48, 44, 40, 36, 32 **7.** 72, 68, 64, 60, 56, 52 **8.** 20, 16,12, 8, 4, 0
9. 96, 92, [88], 84, 80, 76 **10.** 40, 36, 32, 28, 24, 20

Counting by 5s and 25s p. 3
1. 10, 15, 20, 25, 30 **2.** 40, 45, 50, 55, 60, 65 **3.** 75, 80, 85, 90, 95, 100 **4.** 30, 25, [20], 15, 10, 5
5. 95, 90, 85, 80, 75, 70 **6.** 65, 60, 55, 50, 45, 40 **7.** 75, 100, 125, 150, 175 **8.** 225, 250, 275, 300, 325, 350
9. 275, 250, 225, 200, 175

Counting by 10s p. 4
1. 30, 40, 50, [60], 70, 80 **2.** 43, 53, 63, 73, 83, 93 **3.** 234, 244, 254, 264, 274, 284 **4.** 59, 69, 79, 89, 99, 109
5. 140, 150, 160, 170, 180, 190 **6.** 90, 80, 70, 60, 50, 40 **7.** 71, 61, 51, 41, 31, 21 **8.** 158, 148, 138, 128, 118, 108
Brain Stretch **a)** 20 **b)** 30 **c)** 50 **d)** 70

Counting by 100s p. 5
1. 300, 400, 500, 600, 700 **2.** 402, 502, [602], 702, 802, 902 **3.** 315, 415, 515, 615, 715, 815, 915
4. 227, 327, 427, 527, 627, 727 **5.** 448, 548, 648, 748, 848, 948 **6.** 800, 700, 600, 500, 400, 300
7. 643, 543, 443, 343, 243, 143 **8.** 519, 419, 319, 219, 119, 19
Brain Stretch **a)** 300 **b)** 500 **c)** 1000

Counting Back by 5s p. 6
Brain Stretch **a)** 50 was the mistake, it should have been 52 **b)** 88 was the mistake, it should have been 87
c) 61 is the mistake, it should have been 60

Counting by 25s to 1000 p. 7
Brain Stretch **a)** 870, 865, 860, 855, 850, 845, 840 **b)** 934, 924, 914, 904, 894, 884, 874

Growing Number Patterns p. 8
1. 12, 16, 20, 24, 28, 32, 36 **2.** 20, 25, 30, 35, 40, 45, 50 **3.** 15, 25, 35, 45, 55, 65, 75 **4.** Various answers possible depending on which number the student chooses to add each time. Example answer: student chooses to add 3. Pattern continues as 9, 12, 15, 18, 21, 24, 27

Shrinking Number Patterns p. 9
1. 27, 24, 21, 18, 15, 12, 9 **2.** 40, 35, 30, 25, 20, 15, 10 **3.** 80, 70, 60, 50, 40, 30, 20 **4.** Various answers possible depending on which number the student chooses to subtract each time. Example answer: student chooses to subtract 3. Pattern continues as 22, 19, 16, 13, 10, 7, 4

Odd and Even Numbers p. 10
Odd: 23, 715, 689, 991, 375, 675, 807, 5, 777, 51, 11, 93. Even: 904, 34, 2, 74, 70, 536, 352, 44, 12, 678, 68.

Comparing and Ordering Numbers p. 11

1. Just before: 55, Just after: 22, Just before and after: 79, [89], 99 , Between: 24, Just after: 36
2. a) 231 **b)** 345 **c)** 129 **d)** 320 **e)** 537 **f)** 456 **g)** 959 **h)** 222 **3.** 111, 118, 127, 129, 154, 171; 30, 317, 339, 363, 384, 400
4. 123, 95, 84; 289, 245, 212

Hundreds, Tens, and Ones pp. 12–13

1. 2, 1, 8; 218 **2.** 3, 1, 9; 319 **3.** 1, 3, 7; 137 **4.** 5, 3, 0; 530 **5.** 2, 3, 3; 233 **6.** 3, 4, 5; 345
7. 1, 4, 5; 145 **8.** 2, 3, 1; 231 **9.** 3, 2, 2; 322 **10.** 4, 1, 5; 415 **11.** 5, 0, 4; 504 **12.** 2, 5, 5; 255
Brain Stretch **a)** 149 should be circled. **b)** 128 should be circled. **c)** 289 should be circled. **d)** 475 should be circled.

Writing the Number p. 14

1. 6, 4, 3, 643 **2.** 3, 5, 0, 350 **3.** 1, 6, 7, 167 **4.** 5, 3, 9, 539

Place Value p. 15

2. 20 **3.** 400 **4.** 80 **5.** 200 **6.** 70 **7.** 500 **8.** 2 **9.** 400 + 70 + 6 **10.** 200 + 50 + 8
11. 900 + 60 + 7

What Is the Value? p. 16

1. 9 **2.** 3 **3.** 1 **4.** 7 **5.** 40 **6.** 4 **7.** 70 **8.** 2
Brain Stretch **a)** > **b)** > **c)** < **d)** <

Writing Numbers in Different Ways p. 17

1. 140 + 1, blocks image **2.** blocks image, 2 hundreds and 2 tens and 9 ones
3. 3 hundreds and 1 ten and 6 ones, 300 + 10 + 6 **4.** blocks image, 1 hundred and 5 tens and 3 ones
5. 2 hundreds and 9 tens and 0 ones, 200 + 90 + 0 **6.** 300 + 60 + 5, 3 hundreds + 6 tens + 5 ones

Writing Numbers in Standard Form p. 18

1. 145 **2.** 76 **3.** 92 **4.** 262 **5.** 304 **6.** 211 **7.** 856 **8.** 80 **9.** 650 **10.** 45
11. 439 **12.** 583

Writing Number Words p. 19

1. b) two hundred thirty-four **c)** four hundred fifty-six **d)** one hundred thirty-nine **e)** nine hundred eighteen
2. a) twelve **b)** fifty-two **c)** three hundred sixty-five **d)** thirty, thirty-one **e)** twenty-four **f)** sixty

Number Round Up p. 20

1. 670, 700 **2.** 100, 100 **3.** 840, 800 **4.** 110, 100 **5.** 650, 700 **6.** 720, 700 **7.** 570, 600 **8.** 450, 500 **9.** 500, 500 **10.** 810, 800

Ordinal Numbers p. 21

1. 1st, 2nd, 3rd, 4th, 5th, 6th, 7th, 8th, 9th, 10th **2. a)** a **b)** d **c)** o **d)** h **e)** n **3. a)** Louis **b)** Lisa **c)** fifth **d)** eleventh

Adding or Subtracting p. 22

First Row: 29, 19, 11 Second Row: 22, 27, 20 Third Row: 13, 21, 28 Fourth Row: 21, 25, 18 Fifth Row: 25, 22, 7
Sixth Row: 19, 27, 6

Three-Digit Addition Without Regrouping pp. 23–24

1. First Row: 685, 637, 698, 897, 974 Second Row: 962, 788, 685, 595, 946 Third Row: 987, 657, 864, 899, 744
Fourth Row: 797, 952, 448, 833, 695 **2.** First Row: 147, 785, 713, 478, 497 Second Row: 357, 948, 488, 854, 956
Third Row: 348, 598, 976, 566, 858 Fourth Row: 753, 376, 999, 979, 866 Fifth Row: 599, 879, 849, 948, 998

Three-Digit Addition with Regrouping pp. 25–26
1. 819, 713, 747, 729, 327, 407, 817, 835, 609, 809, 929, 917, 318, 615, 809
2. [651], 697, 680, 771, 854, 574, 850, 772, 991, 686, 766, 865, 853, 670, 781 **3.** [402], 415, 623, 821, 814

Taking Apart to Make Tens for Addition p. 27
1. a) 8 + 2 + 5, 10 + 5, 15 **b)** 25 + 5 + 4, 30 + 4, 34 **2. a)** 34 + 6 +1 = 40 + 1 = 41 **b)** 49 + 1 + 3 = 50 + 3 = 53 **c)** 73 + 7 + 1 = 80 + 1 = 81 **d)** 59 + 1 + 4 = 60 + 4 = 64 **e)** 48 + 2 + 11 = 50 + 11 = 50 + 10 + 1 = 61 **f)** 65 + 5 + 10 = 70 + 10 = 80

Three-Digit Subtraction Without Regrouping pp. 28–29
1. 247, 244, 116, 144, 321, 455, 264, 212, 144, 471, 322, 526, 110, 111, 20, 455, 202, 75, 151, 303
2. 12, 716, 442, 14, 264, 127, 157, 325, 213, 210, 214, 101, 145, 216, 315, 211, 73, 343, 152, 863
Brain Stretch 113

Subtraction Match p.30
245 – 131 = 114, 396 – 252 = 144, 697 – 30 = 667, 528 – 212 = 316, 473 – 222 = 251, 138 – 35 = 103, 779 – 348 = 431, 484 – 162 = 322

Taking Apart to Make Tens for Subtraction pp. 31–32
1. a) 16 – 10 = 6 **b)** 13 + 3 – 7 + 3 = 16 – 10 = 6, add 3 **c)** 17 + 2 – 8 + 2 = 19 – 10 = 9, add 2 **d)** 18 + 1 – 9 + 1 = 19 – 10 = 9, add 1 **e)** 43 + 4 – 6 + 4 = 47 – 10 = 37, add 4 **f)** 34 + 5 – 5 + 5 = 39 – 10 = 29, add 5 **g)** 26 + 3 – 7 + 3 = 29 – 10 = 19, add 3 **2. a)** 34 + 3 – 17 + 3 = 37 – 20 = 17, add 3 **b)** 28 + 1 – 19 + 1 = 29 – 20 = 9, add 1 **c)** 22 + 4 – 16 + 4 = 26 – 20 = 6, add 4 **d)** 34 + 5 – 15 + 5 = 39 – 20 = 19, add 5 **e)** 43 + 5 – 35 + 5 = 48 – 40 = 8. Add 5 **f)** 51 + 1 – 39 + 1 = 52 – 40 = 12, add 1 **g)** 35 + 4 – 26 + 4 = 39 – 30 = 9, add 4

Three-Digit Subtraction with Regrouping pp. 33–34
1. 191, 181, 371, 263, 292, 80, 190, 180, 281, 182, 482, 493, 360, 591, 461 **2.** [311], 295, 219, 118, 515, 215, 112, 307, 208, 161, 559, 113, 336, 145, 219 **3.** 234, 245, 637, 95, 256

Word Problems p. 35
1. 49, subtract **2.** 107, subtract **3.** 432, add **4.** 693, add

Money Riddle p. 36
When there is change in the weather.

Counting with Coins p. 37
1. $3.75 **2.** $5.25 **3.** $4.25 **4.** $5.50 **5.** $4.75

Estimating Coins p. 38
1. Estimate could vary, $2.50 **2.** Estimate could vary, $4.35 **3.** Estimate could vary, $3.50 **4.** Estimate could vary, $4.75

Trading Coins p. 39
1. a) $1.75, $1.00 + $0.25 + $0.25 + $0.25 **b)** $2.15, $2.00 + $0.10 + $0.05 **c)** $2.30, $2.00 + $0.25 + $0.05 **d)** $3.10, $2.00 + $1.00 + $0.10

Comparing Money Values pp. 40–41
1. a) $7.05 > $3.55 **b)** $7.90 > $6.65
Brain Stretch **1.** $4.50 **2.** $9.45 **3.** $2.25
2. a) $8.00 > $7.65 **b)** $8.35 > $7.30 **c)** $7.15 < $8.15

At the Cafeteria p. 42

1. \$0.65, \$0.85, \$0.90, \$0.95,\$1.15, \$1.50, \$1.80, \$1.90 **2. a)** \$3.00 **b)** Yes **3.** Answers may vary, but should not exceed \$4.75. Example: Amin could buy a sandwich, macaroni and cheese, and a lemonade. \$4.75 – \$1.90 – \$1.80 – \$0.95 = \$0.10 change **4.** Answers may vary, but should not exceed \$6.00. Example: With \$6.00 you could buy a sandwich, macaroni and cheese, a pizza slice, and jello, and have \$0.15 leftover.

Arrays pp. 43–44

1. a) 4, 5, 4 × 5 = 20 **b)** 3, 6, 3 × 6 = 18 **c)** 3, 4, 3 × 4 = 12 **2. a)** 2 × 5 = 10 **b)** 5 × 2 = 10 **c)** 3 × 5 = 15 **d)** 3 × 3 = 9 **3. a)** 5 × 3 = 15 **b)** 4 × 6 = 24 **c)** 1 × 5 = 5 **d)** 2 × 7 = 14 **e)** 3 × 4 = 12 **f)** 6 × 2 = 12 **g)** 4 × 4 = 16 **h)** 6 × 1 = 6 **i)** 3 × 2 = 6 **j)** 7 × 4 = 28 **k)** 2 × 5 = 10 **l)** 5 × 5 = 25

Multiplying by Skip Counting p. 45

4 × 5 = 20; 2 × 5= 10; 2 × 9 =18

Skip Counting p. 46

1. 6, 18 **2.** 8, 40 **3.** 5, 50

Addition and Multiplication pp. 47–48

1. 12, 12; 6, 6; 20, 20; 12, 12; 14, 14; 16, 16 **2.** 5 + 5 + 5 = 15, 3 × 5 = 15; 8 + 8 = 16, 2 × 8 = 16; 7 + 7 = 14, 2 × 7 = 14; 3 + 3 + 3 + 3 + 3 = 15, 5 × 3 = 15; 9 + 9 = 18, 2 × 9 = 18; 4 + 4 + 4 + 4 = 16, 4 × 4 = 16; 5 + 5 + 5 + 5 = 20, 4 × 5 = 20; 10 + 10 = 20, 2 × 10 = 20; 2 + 2 + 2 + 2 + 2 = 10, 5 × 2 = 10

Using Doubles to Multiply pp. 49–50

1. 5, 20, 5, 10, 20 + 10 = 30, 30; 7, 20, 7 is 14, 20 + 14 = 34, 34; 4, 20, 4 is 8, 20 + 8 = 28, 28; 1, 40, 1 is 2, 40 + 2 = 42, 42
2. a) 14, 28 **b)** 16, 32 **c)** 10, 20 **d)** 18, 36 **e)** 15, 30 **f)** 18, 36

Match Up Fun p. 51

Column one: 8, 18, 20, 6, 2, 18, 12, 70, 4, 16, 81, 6, 8, 14, 30
Column two: 16, 30, 6, 12, 70, 18, 20, 2, 6, 8, 8, 4, 14, 81, 18

Multiplication Fun p. 52

1. 6 × 6 = 36, 5 × 4 = 20, 2 × 5 = 10, 4 × 3 = 12, 6 × 2=12, 4 × 2 = 8, 3 × 5 = 15, 3 × 3= 9, 4 × 6=24

Multiplication Riddle p. 53

A = 20, E = 18, G = 8, H = 15, I = 14, L = 12, N = 25, R = 6, S = 10, T = 0, U = 4, W = 16, Y = 9; He was getting a little rusty!

Multiplying by 1, 2, and 3 p. 54

First Row: 18, 3, 9, 2, 8, Second Row: 10, 15, 2, 16, 27 Third Row: 6, 4, 0, 6, 3 Fourth Row: 0, 5, 4, 6, 14, Fifth Row: 9, 12, 24

Doubles Plus One More Group p. 55

10, 5, 10 + 5 = 15, 15; 14, 7, 14 + 7 = 21, 21; 12, 6, 12 + 6 = 18, 18

Multiplying by 4, 5, and 6 p. 56

First Row: 24, 4, 54, 12, 20 Second Row: 25, 20, 6, 40, 36 Third Row: 15, 24, 0, 8, 18, Fourth Row: 0, 30, 10, 36, 35
Brain Stretch 32,

Multiplying by 7, 8, and 9 p. 57
First Row: 54, 9, 63, 14, 32 Second Row: 40, 45, 7, 64, 81 Third Row: 24, 28, 0, 18, 21 Fourth Row: 0, 35, 16, 42, 49
Brain Stretch 72, image of 8 groups of 9

Multiplying by 10 p. 58
First Row: 10, 90, 20, 60, 40, Second Row: 50, 30, 70, 100, 80 Third Row: 90, 20, 50, 60, 10, Fourth Row: 0, 70, 40, 30, 100, Fifth Row: 10, 20, 60

Math Joke p. 59
F = 9, W = 70, D = 45, T = 8, I = 25, Y = 40, S = 64, E = 27, M = 30, A = 36, L = 4, N = 12, H = 16, O = 100;
He wanted to see time fly!
Brain Stretch 8, 9, 7, 8

Introducing Division p. 60
1. 5, 5 **2.** 4, 4 **3.** 4, 4 **4.** 2, 2 **5.** 4, 4

Dividing by Skip Counting p. 61
18; 8, 16, 8; 3, 5, 15, 3; 5, 4, 20, 5

Division Fun p. 62
1. 12 ÷ 4 = 3 **2.** 10 ÷ 2 = 5 **3.** 12 ÷ 6 = 2 **4.** 10 ÷ 2 = 5 **5.** 8 ÷ 2 = 4 **6.** 8 ÷ 4 = 2

Division Riddle p. 63
A = 2, B = 6, D = 3, L = 4, N = 7, O = 5, S = 8, T = 1, U = 9; Nuts and bolts!
Brain Stretch 40 ÷ 8 = 5, 5 rows of eight trees.

Relating Addition and Division p. 64
1. 12, 3, 4, 12 **2.** 27, 9, 3, 27 **3.** 50, 5, 10, 50 **4.** 10, 2, 5, 5 **5.** 24, 4, 6, 24 **6.** 32, 8, 4, 8 **7.** 30, 6, 5, 30 **8.** 16, 8, 2, 2 **9.** 40, 8, 5, 5 **10.** 20, 5, 4, 5

Related Facts p. 65
First Row; 5, 2, 3, Second Row: 1, 5, 2, Third Row: 1, 4, 1, Fourth Row: 5, 12, 7, Fifth Row: 4, 3, Sixth Row: 18, 40

Dividing by 1, 2, and 3 p. 66
First Row: 6, 1, 7, 4, 6, Second Row: 5, 7, 1, 1, 2, Third Row: 5, 2, 9, 3, 3, Fourth Row: 2, 9, 9, 8, 8, Fifth Row: 5, 8, 6, 4, 5

Dividing by 4, 5, and 6 p. 67
First Row: 10, 9, 8, 4, 5 Second Row: 7, 6, 1, 9, 5, Third Row: 8, 3, 10, 2, 5, Fourth Row: 8, 6, 4, 2, 2, Fifth Row: 3, 7, 7, 2, 4

Dividing by 7, 8, and 9 p. 68
First Row: 9, 2, 5, 7, 10 Second Row: 2, 4, 8, 7, 7, Third Row: 5, 2, 3, 6, 4, Fourth Row: 9, 8, 6, 1, 9, Fifth Row: 5, 3, 1, 2, 4

Dividing by 10 p. 69
First Row: 8, 6, 1, 4, 2, Second Row: 5, 10, 9, 1, 7, Third Row: 2, 6, 3, 4, 2, Fourth Row: 8, 7, 10, 5, 9

Fractions: Equal Parts p. 70
1. [1/2], 1/4, 1/2 **2.** 1/4, 1/2, 1/2 **3.** 1/3, 1/2, 1/2 **4.** 1/4, 1/2, 1/4 **5.** 1/8, 1/4, 1/2 **6.** 1/2, 1/3,1/3

Exploring Fractions pp. 71–72
1. 7/8, 1/8, 1/2, 2/6, 3/5, 8/9, 3/4, 2/3, 1/3. Brain Stretch: 1. c, 2. c
2. 1/8, 2/3, 2/3, 5/6, 2/5, 4/10, 1/2, 2/9, 3/9, 2/8, 1/2, 3/4. Brain Stretch: **a)** 3/11 **b)** 2/5.

Colouring Fractions p. 73
Answers will vary
Brain Stretch Answers will vary

Fractions as Part of a Group p. 74
One image should be coloured, two of the images should be coloured, 2 of the images should be coloured, one of the images should be coloured, 3 of the images should be coloured, one of the images should be coloured, one of the images should be coloured, one of the images should be coloured.

Fraction Problems p. 75
1. 2/4 **2.** 3/8 **3.** 1/3 **4.** 2/8 **5.** 1/2

Exploring Polygons pp. 76–78
triangle: 3, 3; square: 4, 4; pentagon: 5, 5; hexagon: 6, 6; octagon: 8, 8; rectangle: 4, 4; rhombus: 4, 4; parallelogram: 4, 4; trapezoid: 4, 4
Brain Stretch Answers may vary.
1.1, 3, 5, 8, 10, 11, and 14 should all be crossed out. 7, should be coloured blue.
2, 4, 6, 9, 12, 13, and 15 should be coloured red.
Brain Stretch 1, 3, 4, 5, 7, and 9 should be coloured orange. 2, 6, 8, and 10 should be crossed out.

2D Shapes p. 79
rhombus, hexagon, circle, triangle, octagon, pentagon, trapezoid, rectangle, parallelogram, oval, square

Sorting 2D Shapes p. 80
The pentagon and hexagon should be coloured. The square, rectangle, and trapezoid should be coloured.
The square, triangle, and trapezoid should be coloured. The pentagon, rectangle, and octagon should be coloured.
The rectangle, circle, triangle, and parallelogram should be coloured.

2D Shapes p. 81
5; 4, 3; 1, 6, 8, 9, 10; 9, 10; 1, 4, 3, 8, 9, 10

Identifying 3D objects pp. 82–83
1. The objects in the left hand column are as follows: pyramid, cube, cylinder, cone, sphere, rectangular prism.
2. The gift should be circled. The can should be circled. The ball should be circled.
Brain Stretch **a)** The cube should be circled. **b)** the cylinder should be circled.

Attributes of 3D Objects p. 84
Sphere, 1, 0, 0 Cube, 6, 12, 8 Cylinder, 3, 2, 0 Cone, 2, 1, 1

3D Objects p. 85
1. Cube should be circled. **2.** Cone should be circled. **3.** Rectangular Prism should be circled.
4. Square-based pyramid should be circled. **5.** Triangular pyramid should be circled. **6.** Cylinder should be circled.
7. Triangle-based prism should be circled. **8.** Cube should be circled.

Exploring Symmetry p. 86
M, C, E, O, U, and X should be circled. B, Q, and K should be crossed out.

Symmetry Fun p. 87
Student artwork will vary, but should be symmetric to the left half of the ship.

Congruent Figures p. 88
Brain stretch 1, 0, 1, 0, 0

Flips, Slides, and Turns p. 89
1. Flip **2.** Slide **3.** Turn **4.** Slide **5.** Turn

Exploring Pictographs p. 90
1. Strawberry Pie **2.** 14 **3.** 36

Exploring Bar Graphs p. 91
1. 43 children voted altogether. **2.** Strawberry and rocky road were equally the most popular flavours. **3.** Mint chip and other were the least popular flavours. **4.** Strawberry and rocky road got the same number of votes, as did mint chip and other. **5.** 1 More child liked strawberry than chocolate.

Exploring Bar Graphs p. 92
1. Basketball **2.** Baseball **3.** 6 **4.** 2 more people liked tag

Exploring Bar Graphs p. 93
1. veggie **2.** veggie and pepperoni. **3.** other **4.** 100 **5.** various answers

Reading Tally Charts p. 94
1. chocolate chip **2.** 11 **3.** Animal Crackers **4.** 45 **5.** 7 **6.** 15 **7.** 18

Favourite Snacks Graph p. 95
1. Crackers **2.** Veggies **3.** 4 **4.** 11 **5.** 47

Favourite Recess Activities Graph p. 96
3. Baseball **4.** Basketball **5.** 42 **6.** Answers could be: Baseball more than skipping or baseball more than basketball or skipping more than basketball.

Favourite Vegetables Bar Graph p. 97
1. Broccoli **2.** 3 **3.** Lettuce, cucumber, carrots, green beans, broccoli. **4.** 10 **5.** 32 **6.** 27

Exploring Ordered Pairs pp. 98–99
1. b) (2,2) **c)** (4,9) **d)** (9,3) **e)** (7, 6) **f)** (4,4)

Exploring Measurement p. 100
1. metre, centimetre, kilometre, centimetre, centimetre, metre
2. amount matches to measuring cup, weight matches to scale, temperature matches to thermometer, length matches to ruler.

Exploring Perimeter p. 101
4m + 6m + 8m = 18m; 9m + 2m + 9m + 2m = 22m; 4m + 3m + 1m + 3m = 11m; 4m + 4m + 4m + 4m = 16m

Exploring Perimeter p. 102

1. 14 **2.** 12 **3.** 12 **4.** 18

Brain Stretch Figure a should be circled.

Exploring Area pp. 103–104

1. a) 7 **b)** 12 **c)** 9 **d)** 10 **e)** 7 **f)** 10 **2. a)** 10 **b)** 6 **c)** 10 **d)** 8 **e)** 16 **f)** 10 **g)** 10 **h)** 7 **i)** 10

Exploring Length p. 105

1. 6cm **2.** 10cm **3.** 3cm **4.** 9cm

What Time Is It? p. 106

1. 9:30 **2.** 3:20 **3.** 5:30 **4.** 10:50 **5.** 8:15 **6.** 12:35

Drawing the Hands p. 107

See student's work.

Elapsed Time p. 108

1. 3:40, 4:35, 55 **2.** 12:30, 1:30, 1 **3.** 4:15, 6:20, 2, 5

Basketball Fun p. 109

2. 175 minutes

Brain Stretch **a)** 5:40pm **b)** 6:50pm

Using a Schedule p. 110

1. The dolphin show and the shark show. **2.** The exotic fish tour, and the underwater movie show.

3. The aquarium show and the whale show. **4.** Answers may vary. Check to see that show times do not overlap.

Reading a Calendar p. 111

1. Monday **2.** Five **3.** March 12th **4.** March 1 **5.** Friday **6.** March 21st **7.** June 10th

8. June 25th **9.** June 16th **10.** June 26th

Printed in the USA
CPSIA information can be obtained
at www.ICGtesting.com
LVHW081759271123
765061LV00015B/840

9 780978 075620